Collateral Damage

Collateral Damage

Social Inequalities in a Global Age

Zygmunt Bauman

polity

First published in 2011 by Polity Press
Reprinted 2011 (twice), 2012 (three times), 2014

Polity Press
65 Bridge Street
Cambridge CB2 1UR, UK

Polity Press
350 Main Street
Malden, MA 02148, USA

ISBN-13: 978-0-7456-5294-8
ISBN-13: 978-0-7456-5295-5(pb)

A catalogue record for this book is available from the British Library.

Typeset in 11 on 13 pt Sabon
by Toppan Best-set Premedia Limited
Printed and bound in Great Britain by TJ International Limited, Padstow, Cornwall

The publisher has used its best endeavours to ensure that the URLs for external websites referred to in this book are correct and active at the time of going to press. However, the publisher has no responsibility for the websites and can make no guarantee that a site will remain live or that the content is or will remain appropriate.

Every effort has been made to trace all copyright holders, but if any have been inadvertently overlooked the publisher will be pleased to include any necessary credits in any subsequent reprint or edition.

For further information on Polity, visit our website: www.politybooks.com

Contents

Introduction: Collateral damage of social inequality

The moment an electrical power circuit becomes overloaded, the first part to go bust is the fuse. The fuse, an element unable to sustain as much voltage as the rest of the wiring (in fact the *least resistant* part of the circuit), was inserted in the network deliberately; it will melt before any other segment of the wiring does, at the very moment when the electric current increases beyond a safe tension, and so before it manages to put the whole circuit out of operation, along with the peripherals it feeds. That means that the fuse is a safety device that protects other parts of the network from burning out and falling permanently out of use and beyond repair. But it also means that the workability and endurance of the whole circuit – and therefore the power it can absorb and the amount of work it can do – cannot be greater than the power of resistance of its fuse. Once the fuse goes, the whole circuit stops working.

A bridge does not break down and collapse once the load it carries transcends the average strength of its spans; it collapses much earlier, the moment the weight of the load goes over the carrying capacity of *one* of its spans – its *weakest*. The 'average carrying power' of pillars is a statistical fiction of little if any practical impact on the bridge's usability, just as the 'average strength' of its chain links is of no use in calculating how much pull the chain can survive. Calculating, counting on and going by the averages is in fact the surest recipe for losing both the load and the chain on which it was hung. It does not matter how strong the rest of the spans and their supporting pillars are – it is the weakest of the spans that decides the fate of the whole bridge.

These simple and obvious truths are taken into account whenever a structure of any sort is designed and tested by properly schooled and experienced engineers. They are also well remembered by the operators responsible for servicing structures already installed: in a structure correctly monitored and well looked after, repair works would normally start the moment the endurance of *just one* of the parts falls below the minimal standard of required endurance. I said 'normally' – since alas this rule does not apply to all structures. About the structures that for one reason or another have been exempted from that rule, like poorly attended dams, neglected bridges, shoddily repaired aircraft or hastily and perfunctorily inspected public or residential buildings, we learn *after* the disaster has struck: when it comes to counting the human victims of neglect and the exorbitant financial costs of restoration. One structure, however, stands out far above the rest in the degree to which all the simple, indeed commonsense, truths spelled out above are forgotten or suppressed, ignored, played down or even openly denied: the structure in question is *society*.

In the case of society, it is widely, though wrongly, assumed that the quality of the whole can and ought to be measured by the average quality of its parts – and that if any of its parts falls below the average it might badly affect that particular part, but hardly the quality, viability and operational capacity of the whole. When the state of society is checked and evaluated, it is 'averaged up' indices of income, living standards, health, etc., that tend to be calculated; the extent to which such indices vary from one segment of society to another, and the width of the gap separating the top segments from the lowest, are seldom viewed as relevant indicators. The rise in inequality is hardly ever considered as a signal of other than a financial problem; and in the relatively rare cases when there is a debate about the dangers that inequality portends to the society as a whole, it is more often than not about threats to 'law and order', and not about the perils to such paramount ingredients of society's overall well-being as, for instance, the bodily and mental health of the whole population, the quality of its daily life, the tenor of its political engagement and the strength of the bonds that integrate it into society. In fact, the sole index treated routinely as a measure of well-being, and the criterion of the success or failure of the authorities charged with monitoring and protecting the nation's capacity to stand up to challenges, as well as the nation's ability to resolve the problems it collectively confronts, is the average income or average wealth of its members, not the extent of inequality in income or wealth distribution. The message conveyed by such a choice is that inequality, in itself, is neither a danger to society as a whole, nor a source of the problems that affect society as a whole.

Much of the nature of present-day politics can be explained by the desire of the political class, shared by a substantial part of its electorate, to force reality to obey the above position. A salient symptom of that desire, and of the policy aimed at its fulfilment, is the way the part of the population at the bottom end of the social distribution of wealth and income is encapsulated in the imagined category of the 'underclass': a congregation of individuals who, unlike the rest of the population, do not belong to any class – and so in fact do not belong to society. Society is a *class* society in the sense of being a totality in which individuals are included through their class membership, and are expected to join in performing the function which their class has been assigned to perform in and for the 'social system' as a whole. The idea of the 'underclass' suggests neither a function to be performed (as in the case of the 'working' or 'professional' classes), nor a position occupied in the social whole (as in the case of the 'lower', 'middle' or 'upper' classes). The only meaning carried by the term 'underclass' is that of *falling outside* any meaningful, that is function and position oriented, classification. The 'underclass' may be 'in', but it is clearly not 'of' the society: it does not contribute anything that society needs for its survival and well-being; in fact, society would do better without it. The status of the 'underclass', as the name given to it suggests, is one of 'internal émigrés', or 'illegal immigrants', 'aliens inside' – devoid of the rights owed to recognized and acknowledged members of society; in a nutshell, an alien body that does not count among the 'natural' and indispensable parts of the social organism. Something not unlike a cancerous growth, whose most sensible treatment is excision, and short of that an enforced, induced and contrived confinement and/or remission.

Another symptom of the same desire, tightly intertwined with the first, is an ever more evident tendency to reclassify poverty, that most extreme and troublesome sediment of social inequality, as a problem of law and order, calling therefore for measures habitually deployed in dealing with delinquency and criminal acts. It is true that poverty and chronic unemployment or 'jobless work' – casual, short-term, uninvolving and prospectless – correlates with above-average delinquency; in Bradford, for instance, six miles from where I live and where 40 per cent of youngsters live in families without a single person with a regular job, one in ten young people already have police records. Such a statistical correlation, however, does not in itself justify the reclassification of poverty as a criminal problem; If anything, it underlines the need to treat juvenile delinquency as a *social* problem: lowering the rate of youngsters who come into conflict with the law requires reaching to the roots of that phenomenon, and the roots *are* social. They lie in a combination of the consumerist life philosophy propagated and instilled under the pressure of a consumer-oriented economy and politics, the fast shrinking of life chances available to the poor, and the absence for a steadily widening segment of the population of realistic prospects of escaping poverty in a way that is socially approved and assured.

There are two points that need to be made about the case of Bradford, as about so many similar cases spattered all around the globe. First, to explain them adequately by reference to local, immediate and direct causes (let alone to relate them unambiguously to someone's malice aforethought) is by and large a vain effort. Second, there is little that local agencies, however resourceful and willing to act, can do to prevent or remedy them. The links to the Bradford phenomenon extend far beyond the confines of the city. The situation of youth in Bradford is a *collateral casualty* of profit-driven, uncoordinated and uncontrolled globalization.

The term 'collateral casualty' (or damage, or victim) has recently been coined in the vocabulary of military expeditionary forces, and popularized by journalists reporting their actions, to denote unintended, unplanned – and as some would say, incorrectly, 'unanticipated' – effects, which are all the same harmful, hurtful and damaging. Qualifying certain destructive effects of military action as 'collateral' suggests that those effects were not taken into account at the time the operation was planned and the troops were commanded into action; or that the possibility of such effects was noted and pondered, but was nevertheless viewed as a risk worth taking, considering the importance of the military objective – such a view being so much easier (and so much more likely) for the fact that the people who decided about the worthiness of taking the risk were not the ones who would suffer the consequences of taking it. Many a command-giver would try to retrospectively exonerate their willingness to put other people's lives and livelihoods at risk by pointing out that one can't make an omelette without breaking eggs. What is glossed over in such a case is, of course, someone's legitimized or usurped power to decide which omelette is to be fried and savoured and which are the eggs to be broken, as well as the fact that it won't be the broken eggs who savour the omelette . . . Thinking in terms of collateral damage tacitly assumes an *already existing inequality* of rights and chances, while accepting a priori the unequal distribution of the costs of undertaking (or for that matter desisting from) action.

Apparently, risks are untargeted and neutral, their effects being random; in fact, however, the dice in the game of risks are loaded before they are cast. There is a selective affinity between social inequality and the likelihood of becoming a casualty of catastrophes, whether man-made or 'natural', though in both cases the damage is claimed to be unintended and unplanned. Occupying the bottom end of the inequality ladder, and becoming a 'collateral victim' of a human action or a natural disaster, interact the way the opposite poles of magnets do: they tend to gravitate towards each other.

In 2005 Hurricane Katrina hit the shores of Louisiana. In New Orleans and its surroundings, everybody knew that Katrina was coming, and they all had quite enough time to run for shelter. Not all, though, could act on their knowledge and make good use of the time available for escape. Some – quite a few – could not scrape together enough money for flight tickets. They could pack their families into trucks, but where could they drive them? Motels also cost money, and money they most certainly did not have. And – paradoxically – it was easier for their well-off neighbours to obey the appeals to leave their homes, to abandon their property to salvage their lives; the belongings of the well-off were insured, and so Katrina might be a mortal threat to their lives, but not to their wealth. What is more, the possessions of the poor without the money to pay for air tickets or motels might be meagre by comparison with the opulence of the rich, and so less worthy of regret, but they were their *only* effects; no one was going to compensate them for their loss, and once lost they would be lost forever, and all people's life savings would go down with them.

Katrina might not be choosy or class-biased, it might have struck the rich and the poor with the same cool and dull equanimity – and yet that admittedly natural catastrophe did not feel similarly 'natural' to all its victims. Whereas the hurricane itself was not a human product, its *consequences for humans* obviously were. As the Rev. Calvin O. Butts III, pastor of Abyssinian Baptist Church in Harlem, summed it up (and not he alone), 'The people affected were largely poor people. Poor, black people.'[1] At the same time, David Gonzalez, *New York Times* special correspondent, wrote:

> In the days since neighbourhoods and towns along the Gulf Coast were wiped out by the winds and water, there has been a growing sense that race and class are the unspoken markers of who got out and who got stuck. Just as in developing countries where the failures of rural development policies become glaringly clear at times of natural disasters like floods and drought, many national leaders said, some of the United States' poorest cities have been left vulnerable by federal policies.
>
> 'No one would have checked on a lot of the black people in these parishes while the sun shined,' said Mayor Milton D. Tutwiler of Winstonville, Miss. 'So am I surprised that no one has come to help us now? No.'

Martin Espada, an English professor at the University of Massachusetts, observed: 'We tend to think of natural disasters as somehow even-handed, as somehow random. Yet it has always been thus: poor people are in danger. That is what it means to be poor. It's dangerous to be poor. It's dangerous to be black. It's dangerous to be Latino.' And as it happens, the categories listed as particularly exposed to danger tend largely to overlap. There are many of the poor among blacks and among Latinos. Two-thirds of New Orleans residents were black and more than a quarter lived in poverty, while in the Lower Ninth Ward of the city, swept off the face of the earth by flood waters, more than 98 per cent of residents were black and more than a third lived in poverty.

The most badly injured among the victims of that natural catastrophe were the people who had already been the rejects of order and the refuse of modernization well before Katrina struck; victims of order maintenance and economic progress, two eminently human, and blatantly unnatural, enterprises.[2] Long before they found themselves at the very bottom of the list of priority concerns of the authorities responsible for the security of citizens, they had been exiled to the margins of the attention (and the political agenda) of the authorities who were declaring the pursuit of happiness to be a universal human right, and the survival of the fittest to be the prime means to implement it.

A blood-curdling thought: did not Katrina help, even if inadvertently, the desperate efforts of the ailing disposal industry of wasted humans, struggling to cope with the social consequences of the globalization of the production of a 'redundant population' on a crowded (and from the waste-disposal industry's viewpoint, *over*crowded) planet? Was not that help one of the reasons why the need to despatch troops to the afflicted area was not strongly felt until *social* order was broken and the prospect of *social* unrest came close? Which of the 'early warning systems' signalled that need to deploy the National Guard? A demeaning, blood-curdling thought indeed; one would dearly wish to dismiss it as unwarranted or downright fanciful, if only the sequence of events had made it less credible than it was . . .

The likelihood of becoming a 'collateral victim' of any human undertaking, however noble its declared purpose, and of any 'natural' catastrophe, however class-blind, is currently one of the most salient and striking dimensions of social inequality – and this fact speaks volumes about the already low yet still falling status of social inequality inside the contemporary political agenda. While to those who remember the fate of bridges whose strength has been measured by the average strength of its pillars, it also speaks yet more volumes about the troubles that rising inequality within and between societies holds in store for our shared future.

The link between the heightened probability of a 'collateral casualty' fate and a degraded position on the inequality ladder is the result of a convergence between the endemic or contrived 'invisibility' of collateral victims, on the one hand, and the enforced 'invisibility' of the 'aliens inside' – the impoverished and the miserable – on the other. Both categories, even though for varying reasons, are taken out of consideration whenever the costs of a planned endeavour and the risks entailed by its enactment are calculated and evaluated. Casualties are dubbed 'collateral' in so far as they are dismissed as not important enough to justify the costs of their prevention, or simply 'unexpected' because the planners did not consider them worthy of inclusion among the objects of preparatory reconnoitring. For selection among the candidates for collateral damage, the progressively criminalized poor are therefore 'naturals' – branded permanently, as they tend to be, with the double stigma of non-importance and unworthiness. This rule works in police operations against drug pushers and smugglers of migrants, in military expeditions against terrorists, but also for governments seeking additional revenue by opting for increases in VAT and cancelling the extensions of children's playgrounds, rather than through raising taxation on the rich. In all such cases and a growing multitude of others, causing 'collateral damage' comes easier in the rough districts and mean streets of the cities than in the gated shelters of the high and mighty. So distributed, the risks of creating collateral victims may even turn sometimes (and for some interests and purposes) from a liability into an asset . . .

It is that close affinity and interaction between inequality and collateral casualties, the two phenomena of our time that are both growing in volume and importance as well as in the toxicity of the dangers they portend, that are approached, each time from a somewhat different perspective, in the successive chapters of the present volume, based in most cases on lectures prepared and delivered in 2010–11. In some of the chapters the two issues appear in the foreground, in some others they serve as a backdrop. A general theory of their interconnected mechanisms remains yet to be written; this volume can be seen as at best a series of tributaries aiming at an as yet untrailed and uncharted riverbed. I am aware that the work of synthesis still lies ahead.

I am sure, however, that the explosive compound of growing social inequality and the rising volume of human suffering relegated to the status of 'collaterality' (marginality, externality, disposability, not a legitimate part of the political agenda) has all the markings of being potentially the most disastrous among the many problems humanity may be forced to confront, deal with and resolve in the current century.

1

From the agora
to the marketplace

Democracy is the form of life of the *agora*: of that intermediate space which links/separates the two other sectors of the polis: *ecclesia* and *oikos*.

In Aristotle's terminology, oikos stood for the family household, the site within which private interests were formed and pursued; ecclesia stood for the 'public' – for the people's council composed of magistrates, elected, appointed or drawn by lot, whose function was to care for the common affairs affecting all the citizens of the *polis*, such as matters of war and peace, defence of the realm and the rules governing the cohabitation of citizens in the city-state. Having originated from the verb *kalein*, meaning to call, to summon, to gather, the concept of 'ecclesia' presumed from the beginning the presence of the agora, the place for coming to meet and talk, the site of encounter between people and the council: the site of democracy.

In a city-state, the agora was a physical space to which the *boule*, the council, summoned all the citizens (heads of households) once or several times each month to deliberate on and decide issues of joint and shared interests – and to elect, or draw by lot, its members. For obvious reasons, such a procedure could not be sustained once the realm of the polis or the body politic grew far beyond the borders of a city: the agora could no longer literally mean a public square where all the citizens of the state were expected to present themselves in order to participate in the decision-making process. This does not mean, though, that the purpose underlying the establishment of the agora, and the function of the agora in pursuing that purpose, had lost their significance or needed to be abandoned forever. The history of democracy can be narrated as the story of successive efforts to keep alive both the purpose and its pursuit after the disappearance of its original material substratum.

Or one could say that the history of democracy was set in motion, guided and kept on track by the *memory of the agora*. One could, and should, say as well that the preservation and resuscitation of the memory of the agora was bound to proceed along varied paths and take different forms; there is not one exclusive way in which the job of mediation between oikos and ecclesia can be accomplished, and hardly any one model is free from its own hitches and stumbling blocks. Now, more than two millennia later, we need to be thinking in terms of *multiple democracies*.

The *purpose* of the agora (sometimes declared but mostly implicit) was and remains the perpetual coordination of 'private' (oikos based) and 'public' (ecclesia handled) interests. And the *function* of the agora was and still is to provide the essential and necessary condition of such coordination: namely, *the two-way translation between the language of individual/familial interests and the language of public interests*. What was essentially expected or hoped to be achieved in the agora was the reforging of private concerns and desires into public issues; and, conversely, the reforging of issues of public concern into individual rights and duties. The degree of democracy of a political regime may therefore be measured by the success and failure, the smoothness and roughness of that *translation*: to wit, by the degree to which its principal objective has been reached, rather than, as is often the case, by staunch obedience to one or another *procedure*, viewed wrongly as the simultaneously necessary and sufficient condition of democracy – of all democracy, of democracy *as such*.

As the city-state model of 'direct democracy', where an on-the-spot estimate could be made of its success and the smoothness of translation simply by the number of citizens partaking in flesh and voice in the decision-taking process, was clearly inapplicable to the modern, resurrected concept of democracy (and in particular to the 'great society', that admittedly *imagined*, abstract entity, beyond the reach of the citizen's personal experience and impact), modern political theory struggled to discover or invent alternative yardsticks by which the democracy of a political regime could be assessed: indices which could be argued over and shown to reflect and signal that the purpose of the agora had been adequately met and that its function had been properly performed. Most popular perhaps among those alternative criteria have been quantitative ones: the percentage of citizens taking part in the elections which, in 'representative' democracy, replaced the citizens' presence in flesh and voice in the lawmaking process. The effectiveness of such indirect participation tended to be a contentious issue, however, particularly once the popular vote started to turn into the sole acceptable source of rulers' legitimacy, while obviously authoritative, dictatorial, totalitarian and tyrannical regimes tolerating neither public dissent nor open dialogue could easily boast much higher percentages of the electorate at election booths (and so, by formal criteria, much wider popular support for the policies of their rulers) than governments careful to respect and protect *freedom of opinion and expression* – percentages of which the latter could only dream. No wonder that whenever the defining features of democracy are currently spelled out, it is to these criteria of freedom of opinion and expression that the emphases tend to shift from the statistics of electoral attendance and absenteeism. Drawing on Albert O. Hirschman's concepts of 'exit' and 'voice' as the two principal strategies which consumers may deploy (and tend to deploy) in order to gain genuine influence on marketing policies,[1] it has been often suggested that citizens' right to voice their dissent in the open, the provision of means to do so and to reach their intended audience, and the right to opt out from the sovereign realm of a detested or disapproved of regime are the conditions *sine qua non* which political orders must meet to have their democratic credentials recognized.

In the subtitle of his highly influential study, Hirshman puts sellers–buyers and state–citizens relations into the same category, subjected to the same criteria in measuring performance. Such a step was and remains legitimized by the assumption that political freedoms and market freedoms are closely related – needing, as well as breeding and reinvigorating, each other; that the freedom of the markets which underlies and promotes economic growth is in the last account the necessary condition, as well as the breeding ground, of political democracy – while democratic politics is the sole frame in which the economic success can be effectively pursued and achieved. This assumption is, however, contentious, to say the least. Pinochet in Chile, Syngman Rhee in South Korea, Lee Kuan Yew in Singapore, Chiang Kai-shek in Taiwan or the present rulers of China were or are dictators (Aristotle would call them 'tyrants') in everything but the self-adopted names of their offices; but they presided or preside over an outstanding expansion and fast-rising power of markets. All the countries named would not be an epitome of 'economic miracle' today were it not for a protracted 'dictatorship of the state'. And, we may add, it's not just a coincidence that they have become such an epitome.

Let's remember that the initial phase in the emergence of a capitalist regime, the phase of the so-called 'primitive accumulation' of capital, is invariably marked by unprecedented and deeply resented social upheavals, expropriations of livelihoods and a polarization of life conditions; these cannot but shock their victims and produce potentially explosive social tensions, which the up-and-coming entrepreneurs and merchants need to suppress with the help of a powerful and merciless, coercive state dictatorship. And let me add that the 'economic miracles' in postwar Japan and Germany could be explained to a considerable extent by the presence of foreign occupation forces that took over the coercive/oppressive functions of state powers from the native political institutions, while effectively evading all and any control by the democratic institutions of the occupied countries.

One of the most notorious sore spots of democratic regimes is the contradiction between the formal universality of democratic rights (accorded to all citizens equally) and the less than universal ability of their holders to exercise such rights effectively; in other words, the gap separating the legal condition of a 'citizen *de jure*' from the practical capacity of a citizen *de facto* – a gap expected to be bridged by individuals deploying their own skills and resources, which, however, they may – and in a huge number of cases do – lack.

Lord Beveridge, to whom we owe the blueprint for the postwar British 'welfare state', later to be emulated by quite a few European countries, was a *Liberal*, not a socialist. He believed that his vision of comprehensive, collectively endorsed insurance for *everyone* was the inevitable consequence and the indispensable complement of the liberal idea of individual freedom, as well as a necessary condition of *liberal democracy*. Franklin Delano Roosevelt's declaration of war on fear was based on the same assumption, as must also have been Seebohm Rowntree's pioneering inquiry into the volume and causes of human poverty and degradation. Liberty of choice entails, after all, uncounted and uncountable risks of failure; many people would find these risks unbearable, fearing that they might exceed their personal ability to cope. For most people, the liberal ideal of freedom of choice will remain an elusive phantom and idle dream unless the fear of defeat is mitigated by an insurance policy issued in the name of community, a policy they can trust and rely on in the event of personal defeat or a blow of fate.

If democratic rights, and the freedoms that accompany such rights, are granted in theory but unattainable in practice, the pain of hopelessness will surely be topped by the humiliation of haplessness; the ability to cope with life's challenges, tested daily, is after all the very workshop in which the self-confidence of individuals, and so also their self-esteem, is cast or is melted away. Little or no prospect of rescue from individual indolence or impotence can be expected to arrive from a political state that is not, and refuses to be, a *social* state. Without social rights *for all*, a large and in all probability growing number of people will find their political rights of little use and unworthy of their attention. *If political rights are necessary to set social rights in place, social rights are indispensable to make political rights 'real' and keep them in operation.* The two rights need each other for their survival; that survival can only be their *joint* achievement.

The social state has been the ultimate modern embodiment of the idea of *community*: that is, of an institutional reincarnation of that idea in its *modern* form of an '*imagined* totality' – woven of reciprocal dependence, commitment, loyalty, solidarity and trust. Social rights are, so to speak, the tangible, 'empirically given' manifestation of that imagined communal totality (that is, the modern variety of ecclesia, the frame into which democratic institutions are inscribed), which links the abstract notion to daily realities, rooting imagination in the fertile soil of daily life experience. These rights certify the veracity and realism of a mutual person-to-person trust, and of trust in a shared institutional network that endorses and validates collective solidarity.

About sixty years ago T. H. Marshall recycled the popular mood of that time into what he believed had been and was bound to remain a universal law of human progress: from *property* rights to *political* rights, and from them to *social* rights.[2] Political freedom was in his view an inevitable, even if somewhat delayed, outcome of economic freedom, while itself necessarily giving birth to social rights – thereby rendering the exercise of both freedoms feasible and plausible to all. With every successive extension of political rights, so Marshall believed, the agora would grow more inclusive, voice would be given to more and more categories of people hitherto kept inaudible, more and more inequalities would be levelled up, and more and more discriminations effaced. About a quarter of a century later John Kenneth Galbraith spotted another regularity, however, one bound to seriously modify, if not downright refute, Marshall's prognosis: as the universalization of *social* rights begins to bear fruit, more and more holders of *political* rights tend to use their voting entitlements to support the initiative of individuals, with all its consequences: a growing, instead of a diminished or levelled up inequality of incomes, of standards of living and of life prospects. Galbraith ascribed this trend to the sharply different mood and life philosophy of the emergent 'contented majority'.[3] Feeling firm in the saddle now and at home in a world of great risks but also of great opportunities, the emergent majority saw no need for the 'welfare state', an arrangement which they increasingly experienced as a cage rather than a safety net, a constraint rather than an opening – and as wasteful largesse, which they, the contented, able to rely on their own resources and free to roam the globe, would in all probability never need and from which they were unlikely ever to benefit. For them, the local poor, tied fixed to the ground, were no longer a 'reserve army of labour', and money spent on keeping them in good shape was money wasted. The widespread support, 'beyond left and right', for the social state, seen by T. H. Marshall as the ultimate destination of the 'historical logic of human rights', started to shrink, crumble and vanish with accelerating speed.

Indeed, the welfare (social) state would hardly have come to be had not the factory owners once considered the care of a 'reserve army of labour' (keeping the reservists in good shape in case they were called back to active service) to be a profitable investment. The introduction of the social state used indeed to be a matter 'beyond left and right'; now, however, the turn has come for the limitation and gradual dismembering of welfare state provisions to be made into an issue 'beyond left and right'. If the welfare state is now underfunded, falling apart or even being actively dismantled, it is because the sources of capitalist profit have drifted or have been shifted from the exploitation of factory *labour* to the exploitation of *consumers*. And because poor people, stripped of the resources needed to respond to the seductions of consumer markets, need currency and credit accounts (not the kinds of services provided by the 'welfare state') to be of any use in consumer capital's understanding of 'usefulness'.

More than anything else, the 'welfare state' (which, I repeat, is better called a 'social state', a name that shifts the emphasis away from the distribution of material benefits and towards the community-building motive of their provision) was an arrangement invented and promoted as if precisely to prevent the present-day drive to 'privatize' (a shorthand for the promotion of the essentially anti-communal, individualizing patterns of the style of the consumer market, patterns that set individuals in competition with other): a drive that results in a weakening and falling apart of the web of human bonds, thereby undermining the social foundations of human solidarity. 'Privatization' shifts the daunting task of fighting back against and (hopefully) resolving *socially* produced problems onto the shoulders of *individual* men and women, who are in most cases not nearly resourceful enough for the purpose; whereas the 'social state' tends to unite its members in an attempt to protect all and any one of them from the ruthless and morally devastating competitive 'war of all against all'.

A state is 'social' when it promotes the principle of communally endorsed, collective insurance against individual misfortune and its consequences. It is that principle – declared, set in operation and trusted to be working – that lifts an 'imagined society' to the level of a 'genuine totality' – a tangible, sensed and lived community – and thereby replaces (to deploy John Dunn's terms) the 'order of egoism', generating mistrust and suspicion, with the 'order of equality', inspiring confidence and solidarity. And it is the same principle that makes the political body democratic: it lifts members of society to the status of *citizens*, that is, it makes them *stake*holders, in addition to being *stock*holders of the polity; *beneficiaries*, but also *actors* responsible for the creation and decent allocation of benefits. In short, they become citizens defined and moved by their acute interest in their common well-being and responsibility: a network of public institutions that can be trusted to assure the solidity and reliability of the state-issued 'collective insurance policy'. The application of that principle can, and often does, protect men and women from the triple bane of *silencing*, *exclusion* and *humiliation* – most importantly, however, it can (and by and large does) become a prolific source of the social solidarity that recycles 'society' into a common, communal value.

Presently, however, we (the 'we' of the 'developed' countries on our own initiative, as well as the 'we' of the 'developing' countries under the concerted pressure of global markets, the International Monetary Fund and the World Bank) seem to be moving in an opposite direction: 'totalities', societies and communities real or imagined, become increasingly 'absent'. The range of individual autonomy is expanding, but also being burdened with the functions that were once viewed as the responsibility of the state but are now ceded ('subsidiarized') to individual self-concerns. States endorse the collective insurance policy half-heartedly and with mounting reservations, and leave it to individual pursuits to achieve well-being and make it secure.

Not much prompts people, therefore, to visit the agora – and even less prods them to engage in its works. Left increasingly to their own resources and acumen, individuals are expected to devise individual solutions to socially generated problems, and to do it individually, using their individual skills and individually possessed assets. Such an expectation sets individuals in mutual competition, and renders communal solidarity (except in the form of temporary alliances of convenience: that is, of human bonds tied together and untied on demand and with 'no strings attached') to be perceived as by and large irrelevant, if not downright counterproductive. If it is not mitigated by institutional intervention, this 'individualization by decree' renders the differentiation and polarization of individual chances inescapable; indeed, it makes the *polarization* of prospects and chances into a self-propelling and self-accelerating process. The effects of that tendency were easy to predict – and now can be counted. In Britain for instance, the share of the top 1 per cent of earners has doubled since 1982 from 6.5 per cent to 13 per cent of national income, while the chief executives of FTSE 100 companies have been (up to the recent 'credit crunch' and beyond) receiving not 20 as in 1980, but 133 times more than average earners.

This is not, however, the end of the story. Thanks to the network of 'information highways', rapidly growing in extension and density, every and any individual – man or woman, adult or child, rich or poor – is invited, tempted and induced (compelled rather) to compare their own individual lot with the lot of *all other* individuals, and particularly with the lavish consumption practised by public idols (celebrities constantly in the limelight, on TV screens and on the front pages of tabloids and glossy magazines), and to measure the values that make life worth living by the opulence they brandish. At the same time, while the realistic prospects of a satisfying life continue to diverge sharply, the dreamed-of standards and coveted tokens of a 'happy life' tend to converge: the driving force of conduct is no longer the more or less realistic desire to 'keep up with Joneses', but the infuriatingly nebulous idea of 'keeping up with celebrities', catching up with supermodels, premier league footballers and top-ten singers. As Oliver James has suggested, this truly toxic mixture is created by stoking up 'unrealistic aspirations, and the expectations that they can be fulfilled'; but great swathes of the British population 'believe that they can become rich and famous', that 'anyone can be Alan Sugar or Bill Gates, never mind that the actual likelihood of this occurring has diminished since the 1970s'.[4]

The state today is less and less able, and willing, to promise its subjects existential security ('freedom from fear', as Franklin Delano Roosevelt famously phrased it, invoking his 'firm belief' that 'the only thing we have to fear is fear itself'). To a steadily growing extent, the task of gaining existential security – obtaining and retaining a legitimate and dignified place in human society and avoiding the menace of exclusion – is now left to the skills and resources of each individual on his or her own; and that means carrying the enormous risks, and suffering the harrowing uncertainty which such tasks inevitably entail. The fear which democracy and its offspring, the social state, promised to uproot has returned with a vengeance. Most of us, from the bottom to the top, nowadays fear the threat, however unspecified and vague, of being excluded, proved inadequate to the challenge, snubbed, refused dignity and humiliated . . .

On the diffuse and misty fears that saturate present-day society, politicians as much as the consumer markets are eager to capitalize. The merchandizers of consumer goods and services advertise their commodities as foolproof remedies against the abominable sense of uncertainty and ill-defined threats. Populist movements and populist politicians pick up the task abandoned by the weakening and disappearing social state, and also by much of whatever remained of the by and large bygone social-democratic left. But in stark opposition to the social state, they are interested in *expanding* not *reducing* the volume of fears; and particularly in expanding fears of the kinds of dangers which TV can show them to be gallantly resisting, fighting back against and protecting the nation from. The snag is that the menaces most vociferously, spectacularly and insistently displayed by the media seldom, if ever, happen to be the dangers that lie at the roots of popular anxiety and fears. However successful the state might be in resisting the advertised threats, the genuine sources of anxiety, of that ambient and haunting uncertainty and social insecurity, those prime causes of fear endemic to the modern capitalist way of life, will remain intact and, if anything, emerge reinforced.

As far as the bulk of the electorate is concerned, political leaders, present and aspiring, are judged by the severity they manifest in the course of the 'security race'. Politicians try to outdo each other in promises of being tough on the culprits of insecurity – genuine or putative, but those which are near, within reach, and can be fought and defeated, or at least can be deemed to be conquerable and presented as such. Parties like Forza Italia or the Lega Nord may win elections by promising to protect the hardworking Lombardians against being robbed by lazy Calabrians, to defend both against newcomers from foreign lands who remind them of the shakiness and incurable frailty of their own position, and to defend every and any voter against obtrusive beggars, stalkers, prowlers, muggers, car thieves and, of course, gypsies. The snag is that the most awesome threats to decent human life and dignity, and thus to democratic life, will emerge from all that unscathed.

All the same, the risks to which democracies are currently exposed are *only partly* due to the way state governments desperately seek to legitimize their right to rule and to demand discipline by flexing their muscles and showing their determination to stand firm in the face of the endless, genuine or putative, threats to human bodies – instead of (as they did before) protecting their citizens' social usefulness, respected places in society, and insurance against exclusion, the denial of dignity and humiliation. I say 'partly', because the second cause of democracy being at risk is what can only be called 'freedom fatigue', manifested in the placidity with which most of us accept the process of the step-by-step limitation of our hard-won liberties, our rights to privacy, to defence in court, to being treated as innocent until proven guilty. Laurent Bonelli recently coined the term 'liberticide' to denote that combination of states' new and far-fetched ambitions and citizens' timidity and indifference.[5]

A while ago, I watched on TV thousands of passengers stranded at British airports during another 'terrorist panic', when flights were cancelled after an announcement that the 'unspeakable dangers' of a 'liquid bomb' and a worldwide conspiracy to explode aircrafts in flight had been discovered. Those thousands grounded by cancellations lost their holidays, important business meetings, family reunions. But they did not complain! Not in the least . . . Neither did they complain of having been sniffed all over by dogs, kept in endless queues for security checks, submitted to body searches they would normally consider outrageously offensive to their dignity. On the contrary, they were jubilant, and beaming with gratitude: 'We have never felt so safe as now,' they kept repeating, 'we are so grateful to our authorities for their vigilance and for taking such good care of our safety!'

At the extreme of the present-day tendency, we learn of prisoners kept incarcerated for years on end without charge in camps like Guantanamo, Abu Ghraib and perhaps in dozens more, kept secret and for that reason still more sinister and less human; what we have learned has caused occasional murmurs of protest, but hardly a public outcry, let alone an effective counteraction. We, the 'democratic majority', console ourselves that all those violations of human rights are aimed at 'them', not 'us' – at different kinds of humans ('between you and me, are they indeed human?!') and that those outrages will not affect us, the decent people. We have conveniently forgotten the sad lesson learned by Martin Niemöller, the Lutheran pastor and a victim of Nazi persecution. First they took the communists, he mused, but I was not a communist, so I kept silent. Then they came after trade unionists, and

as I was not a trade unionist, I said nothing. Then they came after
Jews, but I was not a Jew . . . And after Catholics, but I was not
a Catholic . . . Then they came for me . . . By that time there was
no one left to speak up for anyone.

In an insecure world, security is the name of the game. Security
is the main purpose of the game and its paramount stake. It is a
value that in practice, if not in theory, dwarfs and elbows out of
view and attention all other values – including the values dear to
'us' while suspected to be hated by 'them', and for that reason
declared the prime cause of their wish to harm us as well as of
our duty to defeat and punish them. In a world as insecure as
ours, personal freedom of word and action, the right to privacy,
access to the truth – all those things we used to associate with
democracy and in whose name we still go to war – need to be
trimmed or suspended. Or, at least, this is what is maintained by
the official version, and confirmed by official practice.

The truth – to be neglected only at democracy's peril – is, nevertheless, that *we cannot effectively defend our freedoms here at
home while fencing ourselves off from the rest of the world and
attending solely to our own affairs.*

Class is only one of the historical forms of inequality, the nation-
state only one of its historical frames, and so 'the end of national
class society' (if indeed the era of the 'national class society' has
ended, which is a moot question) does not augur 'the end of social
inequality'. We now need to extend the issue of inequality beyond
the misleadingly narrow area of income per head, to the fatal
mutual attraction between poverty and social vulnerability, to
corruption, to the accumulation of dangers, as well as to humiliation and denial of dignity, that is to the factors which shape
attitudes and conduct and integrate groups (or more correctly, in
their case, *dis*integrate groups), factors fast growing in volume and
importance in the age of the globality of information.

I believe that what lies beneath the present 'globalization of
inequality' is the current repetition, though this time on a planetary scale, of the process spotted by Max Weber in the origins of
modern capitalism and dubbed by him the 'separation of business
from household': in other words, the emancipation of business
interests from all extant socio-cultural institutions of ethically
inspired supervision and control (concentrated at that time in the

family household/workshop and through it in the local community) – and consequently the immunization of business pursuits against all values other than the maximization of profit. With the benefit of hindsight, we can view the present departures as a magnified replica of that original two-centuries-old process. They have the same outcomes: the rapid spread of misery (poverty, a falling apart of families and communities, a tapering and emaciation of human bonds to Thomas Carlyle's 'cash nexus'), and a newly emergent 'no-man's land' (a sort of 'Wild West', as later to be recreated in Hollywood studios) – free from binding laws and administrative supervision and only sporadically visited by itinerant judges.

To cut a long story short: the original secession of business interests was followed by a long and frenetic, uphill struggle by the emergent state to invade, subdue, colonize and eventually 'normatively regulate' that land of the free-for-all, to lay the institutional foundations for the 'imagined community' (dubbed a 'nation'), intended to take over the life-sustaining functions previously performed by households, parishes, craftsmen's guilds and other institutions imposing community values on business, but now fallen from the weakening hands of local communities robbed of their executive power. Today we witness the Business Secession Mark Two: this time it is the turn of the *nation-state* to be assigned the status of 'households' and 'ramparts of parochialism'; to be frowned on, decried and charged as modernization-impeding, irrational and economy-hostile relics.

The essence of the second secession is, just like the essence of the original one, the *divorce between power and politics*. In the course of its struggle to limit the social and cultural damage of the first secession (culminating in the 'glorious thirty' years following the Second World War), the emergent modern state managed to develop institutions of politics and governance made to the measure of the postulated merger of power (*Macht, Herrschaft*) and politics *inside* the territorial union of nation and state. The marriage of power and politics (or rather their cohabitation inside the nation-state) is now ending in a separation verging on divorce, with power partly evaporating upwards into the cyberspace, partly flowing sideways to militantly and ruggedly apolitical markets, and partly 'subsidiarized' (forcibly, 'by decree') to the area of 'life politics' of newly 'enfranchised' (again by decree) individuals.

The outcomes are very much the same as in the case of the original secession; only this time on an incomparably grander scale. Now, however, there is no equivalent of the postulated 'sovereign nation-state' in sight, able (or hoped to be able) to envisage (let alone to implement) a realistic prospect of taming the so far purely negative (destructive, institutions-dismantling, structures-melting) effect of globalization, and of recapturing the forces running amuck, in order to submit them to ethically guided and politically operated control. Thus far, at least ... We now have *power free from politics*, and *politics devoid of power*. Power is already global; politics stays pitifully local. Territorial nation-states are local 'law and order' police precincts, as well as local dustbins and garbage removal and recycling plants for the globally produced risks and problems.

There are valid reasons to suppose that on a globalized planet, with the plight of everyone everywhere determining the plight of all the others while being determined by them, one can no longer assure and effectively protect democracy 'separately': in one country, or even in a few selected countries, as in the case of the European Union. The fate of freedom and democracy in each land is decided and settled on the global stage; and only on that stage can it be defended with a realistic chance of lasting success. It is no longer in the power of any singly acting state, however resourceful, heavily armed, resolute and uncompromising, to defend chosen values at home while turning its back on the dreams and yearnings of those outside its borders. But turning our backs is precisely what we, the Europeans and Americans, seem to be doing, when keeping our riches and multiplying them at the expense of the poor outside.

A few examples will suffice. If 40 years ago the income of the richest 5 per cent of the world's population was 30 times higher than the income of the poorest 5 per cent, 15 years ago it was already 60 times higher, and by 2002 it had reached a factor of 114.

As pointed out by Jacques Attali in *La Voie humaine*,[6] half of world trade and more than a half of global investment benefit just 22 countries, which accommodate a mere 14 per cent of the world's population, whereas the 49 poorest countries inhabited by 11 per cent of the world's population receive between themselves only a 0.5 per cent share of global product – just about the same as the sum of the income of the three wealthiest men on the planet. Ninety per cent of the total wealth of the planet remains in the hands of just 1 per cent of the planet's inhabitants.

Tanzania earns 2.2 billion dollars a year, which it divides among 25 million inhabitants. Goldman Sachs Bank earns 2.6 billion dollars, which is then divided between 161 stockholders.

Europe and the United States spend 17 billion dollars each year on animal food, while according to experts, just 19 billion dollars is needed to save the world's population from hunger. As Joseph Stiglitz reminded the trade ministers preparing for their Mexico meeting,[7] the average European subsidy per cow 'matches the 2 dollars per day poverty level on which billions of people barely subsist', whereas America's cotton subsidies of 4 billion dollars paid to 25,000 well-off farmers 'bring misery to 10 million African farmers and more than offset the US's miserly aid to some of the affected countries'. One occasionally hears Europe and America publicly accusing each other of 'unfair agricultural practices'. But, Stiglitz observes, 'neither side seems to be willing to make major concessions' – whereas nothing short of a major concession would convince others to stop looking at the unashamed display of 'brute economic power by the US and Europe' as anything other than an effort to defend the privileges of the privileged, to protect the wealth of the wealthy and to serve their interests – which, in their opinion, boil down to more wealth and yet more wealth.

If they are to be lifted and refocused at a level higher than the nation-state, the essential features of human solidarity (like the sentiments of mutual belonging and of shared responsibility for a shared future, or the willingness to care for each other's well-being and to find amicable and durable solutions of sporadically inflamed clashes of interest) need an *institutional* framework of opinion-building and will-formation. The European Union aims (and moves, however slowly and haltingly) towards a rudimentary or embryonic form of such an institutional framework, encountering on its way, as its most obtrusive obstacles, the existing nation-states and their reluctance to part with whatever is left of their once fully fledged sovereignty. The current direction is difficult to plot unambiguously, and predicting its future turns is even more difficult, in addition to being unwarranted, irresponsible and unwise.

We feel, guess, suspect what needs to be done. But we cannot know in what shape or form it eventually will be done. We can be pretty sure, though, that the ultimate shape will not be the one we know. It will be – it must be – different from all the ones we've got used to in the past, in the era of nation-building and nation-states' self-assertion. It can hardly be otherwise, as all political institutions currently at our disposal were made to the measure of the *territorial sovereignty* of the nation-state; they resist being stretched to a planetary, supranational scale, and the political institutions serving the self-constitution of the planet-wide human community won't be, can't be, 'the same, only bigger'. If he were to have been invited to a parliamentary session in London, Paris or Washington, Aristotle might perhaps have approved of its procedural rules and have recognized the benefits it offers to people whom its decisions affect, but he would have been baffled when he was told that what he had been shown was '*democracy* in action'. It is not how Aristotle, who coined the term, visualized a 'democratic polis' . . .

We may well sense that the passage from *international* agencies and tools of action to *universal* – global, planetary, humanity-wide – institutions must be and will be a *qualitative*, not merely a *quantitative* change in the history of democracy. So we may ponder, in a worried way, whether the presently available frames of 'international politics' can accommodate the practices of the emergent global polity or indeed serve as their incubator. What about the United Nations, for instance, briefed at its birth to guard and defend the undivided and unassailable sovereignty of the state over its territory? Can the *binding force* of *planetary* laws depend on the agreements (acknowledged as revocable!) of sovereign members of the 'international community' to obey them?

At its earlier stage, modernity raised human integration to the level of *nations*. Before it finishes its job, however, modernity needs to perform one more task, one that is yet more formidable: to raise human integration to the level of *humanity*, inclusive of the whole population of the planet. However hard and thorny that task may prove to be, it is imperative and urgent, because for a planet of universal interdependency it is, literally, a matter of (shared) life or (joint) death. One of the crucial conditions of this task being earnestly undertaken and performed is the creation of a *global equivalent* (not a replica or a magnified copy) of the 'social state' that completed and crowned the previous phase of modern history

– that of the integration of localities and tribes into *nation-states*. At some point, therefore, a resurgence of the essential core of the socialist 'active utopia' – the principle of collective responsibility and collective insurance against misery and ill fortune – will be indispensable, though this time on the global scale, with *humanity as a whole* as its object.

At the stage already reached by the globalization of capital and commodity trade, no governments, singly or even in groups of several, are able to balance the books – and without the books being balanced, the ability of the 'social state' to continue its practice of cutting effectively at the roots of poverty at home is inconceivable. It is also difficult to imagine governments being able, singly or even in groups of several, to impose limits on consumption and raise local taxation to the levels required by the continuation, let alone the further expansion, of social services. Intervention in the markets is indeed badly needed, but will it be a *state* intervention if it does happen, and particularly if, in addition to merely happening, it also brings tangible effects? It looks rather that it will need to be the work of *non*-governmental initiatives, independent of the state and perhaps even dissident in relation to the state. Poverty and inequality, and more generally the disastrous side-effects and 'collateral damage' of global laissez-faire, cannot be effectively dealt with separately from the rest of the planet, in one corner of the globe (unless at the human cost that North Koreans or the Burmese have been forced to pay). There is no decent way in which single or several territorial states may 'opt out' from the global interdependency of humanity. The 'social *state*' is no longer viable; only a 'social *planet*' can take over the functions that social states tried, with mixed success, to perform.

I suspect that the vehicles likely to take us to that 'social planet' are not territorially sovereign states, but rather extraterritorial and cosmopolitan non-governmental organizations and associations; those that reach directly to people in need above the heads of and with no interference from the local 'sovereign' governments . . .

2

Requiem for communism

The vision of communism was conceived and born on the rising tide of the 'solid' phase of modernity.

The circumstances of its birth must have left their marks deeply engraved – because over many years to come, indeed throughout a century and a half, those marks emerged intact from successive trials and tests, proving in the end indelible. From its cradle to its coffin, communism remained a bona fide 'solid modern' phenomenon. Indeed, communism was a most (perhaps *the* most) faithful, devoted and loving child, as well as (at least in its intention) the most zealous pupil among the solid modernity's offspring; the loyal subaltern and dedicated companion-in-arms of modernity in all its successive crusades, and one of the very few devotees remaining loyal to its ambitions and keen to continue its 'unfinished project' even when the historical tide turned the other way and the 'solidifying' ambitions of modernity had been surrendered by most of its faithful, ridiculed or condemned, abandoned and/or forgotten. Unflinchingly devout to the intentions, promises, tenets and canons of solid modernity, communism stayed to the last on a battlefield already vacated by other units of the modern army; though it could not, and did not, outlive the passing of the 'solid phase'. In the new, 'liquid' phase of modernity, communism was bound to find itself an antiquated curiosity, a relic of bygone times, with nothing to offer to the generations born and groomed inside the new era and no sensible riposte to their profoundly altered ambitions, expectations and concerns.

In its original, 'solid' phase, modernity was a response to the growing frailty and impotence of the *ancien régime*. The separation of business from the household delivered a mortal blow to that regime: as an effect of economic activities opting out of households and so also separating themselves from the dense web of communal and associative bonds in which household life was embedded, and with the reconstitution of productive and distributive activities as 'business' pure and simple, swept clean of communal and guild-linked constraints, the spontanous, unselfconscious reproduction of the customary and traditional tissue of ties that supported and sustained the *ancien régime* started to fall apart.

The secession of 'business' took the *ancien régime* by surprise and caught it unprepared for the challenge and manifestly unable do rise to it. Confrontated with the newly emancipated powers of capital, pulverizing or just pushing aside and ignoring the received rules of the game ('melting all solids and profaning all sacreds', as the two hot-headed youngsters from the Rhineland, Karl Marx and Friedrich Engels, would call it with awe and admiration), the socio-political institutions of the *ancien régime* showed themselves abominably impotent. They were neither able to tame, mitigate or regulate the advance of the new forces, nor capable of containing (let alone repairing) the socially devastating consequences, side-effects and 'collateral damage' left in its trail. The extant 'solids' (that is, the traditional, inherited and entrenched forms of life and human cohabitation) have been doubly discredited: as neither able to enforce regularity and predictability on the actions of the new powers, nor capable of trimming down, let alone effectively resisting, their socially damaging impact.

To put it in a nutshell: the past failed the test of time. It emerged from that test blatantly discredited. For sufferers and the onlookers alike, it was clear that it had to be burned or pulverized – and that a site had to be urgently cleared of the debris for a new magnificent edifice to be erected. Daniel Bell, succintly and poignantly, summed up the essence of that 'modern spirit' when he spoke of 'man's self-conscious will to destroy his past and control his future'.[1] Modernity was born as an intention to strike out the legacy, burden and ballast of past contingencies and to start from scratch. Forty years later, Leonidas Donskis would ask, rhetorically:

> Were Le Corbusier's architectural projects and his suggestions to remove from history all existing cities and their old towns not enough, and to remove paint from canvases that would have to be repainted – these great recommendations were enthusiastically given life by the world's most diligent modernizers, the Bolsheviks and Maoists, were they not? Have we not had our fair share of totalitarian movements involved in the persecution and destruction of art?[2]

The destruction of art . . . New art as the act of destruction of the old . . . Architecture, painting and the other fine arts were only following suit as modernity leaped headlong into recasting the totality of human living (whether singly, severally, or all together) into a work of art. Everything in human life was to be constructed anew, to be conceived and given birth again. Nothing was to be exempted a priori, and indeed nothing was, from the human determination to bring about emancipation from the shackles of history through the expedient of 'creative destruction'. And there was nothing that the human potential for creative destructon could not sweep out of its way, or rehash and rebuild, or conjure up *ab nihilo*. As Lenin was to subsequently declare with characteristically modern panache and self-assurance, there were no fortresses which the Bolsheviks could not (and therefore, presumably, would not) capture . . .

The notion of the 'bankruptcy of the *ancien régime*' referred primarily to the dilapidation and splitting asunder of the social fabric – and so to the disintegration of the extant social order, which in the absence of alternatives was perceived as 'order as such': as the sole alternative to chaos and pandemonium. Modernity was a resolute and vigorous reaction to the decay of received structures and the resulting social disorder. What is sometimes called, retrospectively, 'the project of modernity' was a product of widespread, initially scattered and diffuse but increasingly concentrated, cohesive and focused efforts to fight back against an imminent descent into chaos. What was to be described with the benefit of hindsight as the 'birth of modernity' was the drive to replace the musty and rapidly putrefying, outdated and useless 'solids' of yore by other, made-to-order solid structures – though this time, hopefully, structures of a vastly improved quality: solids trusted to be more solid and so more reliable than their discredited antecedents, by reason of having been *purpose-built* and designed in a manner that rendered them resistant to accidents of history and perhaps even immune to all future contingencies.

In its initial, 'solid' phase, modernity set about 'structuring' hitherto haphazard, poorly coordinated and so insufficiently regular processes: constructing 'structures' and imposing them upon random and contingent processes operated by scattered and free-floating forces, let loose, permanently out of control and often running amuck ('structuring' means in its essence a *manipulation of probabilities*: making the occurrence of some events much more probable, while severely reducing the probability of others). In short, modernity set about replacing the inherited solids that failed to preserve the regularity of the human environment with new and improved solids, which, it was hoped, would demonstrate their capacity to generate an orderly, transparent and predictable state of affairs. Modernity was born under the sign of 'Certainty', and under that sign it scored its most spectacular victories. In its initial 'solid' phase, modernity was lived through as a *long march towards order* – that 'order' understood as a realm of certainty and control, and particularly of the certainty that the hitherto irritatingly capricious events would be brought under control and stay there, thereby becoming predictable and amenable to planning.

A long march it was to be, measured and marked by scientific discoveries and technological inventions and anticipated to eliminate one by one all the causes of present turmoil and future disturbance. Admittedly, that march was bound to be protracted; but by no means endless. The trajectory ahead was to lead towards a finishing line. The long march to certainty and the superior kind of security that only certainty could offer was perhaps to be a long, uphill and tortuous struggle, but it would still be a one-off effort and a once-and-for-all accomplishment. It had been tacitly assumed that contingency and randomness, a profusion of accidents and an overall unpredictability of events, were anomalies; they were either departures from well-established norms, or the effects of the human inability to entrench a 'normality' visualized, postulated and designed as a state of equilibrium and regularity.

The task was to lift up and put back on the rails a world that had been derailed by an engine fault or driver's error, or to relay the rails on a tougher and more resistant bed. The purpose of change was to bring the world to a state in which no more change would be called for: the purpose of *movement* was to arrive at a *steady state*. The purpose of *effort* was the state of *rest*, the purpose of *hard labour* was *leisure*.

Scholars of the budding social sciences were busy, just as the writers of utopias were, constructing models of a 'stable state' of society, and/or a self-equilibrating social system; the kind of setting in which every and any further change, were it to happen, would result solely from external and out-of-the-ordinary factors, while the homeostatic contraption built into the properly designed society would do its best to render such changes redundant. There were (or so it was believed) a finite quantity of problems to be tackled and resolved, so that with every problem resolved one less problem would remain to be faced up to; there were so many human needs neglected, uncatered for and yearning for gratification, but with each successive need gratified one less need would remain to be satisfied – until no outstanding task was left to prompt and justify a further intensification of the supply of productive labour. *The mission of progress was to work itself out of a job* ...

All such beliefs were shared by anyone who reflected on the prospects of history and the management of the human future. Or, rather, all such presumptions were the common tools of thinking – the ideas to think with but not about; they hardly ever rose to the level of consciousness and themselves became objects of critical reflection. Those presumptions were interlocked into an axis around which all other thoughts rotated; alternatively, these presumptions could be envisaged as forming the field on which all battles of ideas (or at least all battles that counted) were fought. The stake of the battles was the choice of the shortest, least expensive and least discomforting itinerary to the ultimate destination of progress: to a society in which all human needs are provided for and all problems afflicting humans and their cohabitation are resolved. A society of universal welfare and a comfortable life, and a society with a steady economy stabilized securely at a level adequate to the task of the uninterrupted purveyance of all those services.

It was within that context that the confrontation between the two opposite 'road maps' was staged: it went down in history as the conflict between capitalism and socialism. Promoters of both conceptions took the tripartite modern promise of liberty, equality and brotherhood most seriously – just as they took the presumption of an intimate, unbreakable link between the three. But the socialist variety reprimanded and censured the advocates and practitioners of capitalism, and particularly of the 'laissez-faire' party, the most radical among them, for doing too little or next to nothing to deliver on that promise. Socialists accused the capitalist version of modernity of the double sin of wastefulness and injustice. Wastefulness: the chaotic scramble for profits forcing production to regularly overshoot needs, and a large part of the product therefore to travel straight to rubbish heaps; the kind of prodigality that could be avoided – were the profit factor disabled, needs assessed in advance and production planned accordingly. Injustice: exploited labour systematically robbed of the value created by labour and thereby expropriated of their share in the wealth of the nation. Both banes, so the socialist indictment went, could certainly be repelled and would probably vanish altogether were it not for the private ownership of the means of production, putting the logic of production at loggerheads with the logic of needs satisfaction: that logic by which all production of goods ought to have been guided. Once private property in the means of production, which is bound to subordinate the production of goods to the logic of profit-making, is abolished, the two banes would follow it into oblivion, together with the morbid contradiction between the social nature of production and private managements of its means. In its Marxian form, socialism was anticipated to arrive as a result of the proletarian revolution. Increasingly angry with their continuing impoverishment and indignity, workers would sooner or later rebel, forcing a change in the rules of the game in their (well-earned and deserved) favour . . .

As the years went by, the prospects of a 'proletarian revolution' seemed to recede, however, and looked increasingly remote. The spectre of revolution together with the rise and development of effective self-defence organizations among factory labour nudged the state (viewed as a political representation of the class of factory owners) to impose limitations on the appetites of profit-seekers and on the inhumanity of labour conditions, and the process thereby turned into a 'self-refuting prophecy': the predicted 'proletarian pauperization' failed to materialize. Evidence grew instead of workers settling down, whether gladly or reluctantly, *inside* the capitalist-run society – and effectively pursuing the improvement of their condition and the satisfaction of their class interests within its framework. That tendency set the visible historical trends in stark opposition to the expectations that followed from the Marxian analysis. And that contradiction yearned to be explained if the expectations it dashed were to be salvaged.

Around the turn from the nineteenth to the twentieth century, a long list of explanations were indeed attempted. One most often broached and gaining most influence was the supposed bribery of the 'working-class bourgeoisie', the highly skilled and highly paid part of the industrial labour force, who thanks to their privileges had developed vested interests in the preservation of the status quo and managed to harness working-class organizations, trade unions as well as the budding political parties in the service of those interests. The 'false consciousness' theory – another, yet more influential explanation – dug deeper still, asserting that the overall setting of a capitalist society prevents its underprivileged, deprived and discriminated parts from perceiving the truth about their own condition, and particularly the *causes* of that condition and so also the *possibility of emancipation* from their misery. Such explanations circulated in numerous versions with varying degrees of sophistication, all of them pointing to a similar conclusion, however: namely that there was little chance of a 'proletarian revolution' being initiated, conducted and seen through *by the workers themselves* (now rebranded 'the masses', with more than a tinge of disdain). Lenin would insist that if it was left to its own resources and wisdom, 'the proletariat' could rise no further than to the level of a 'trade-union mentality'; while Lenin's intellectual fellow travellers, topping his political censure with their own highbrow contempt for 'bourgeois philistines', charged 'the masses' with an inborn inability and unwillingness to rise above the level of a stultifying and stupefying 'mass culture'.

This was the context, stretching between late nineteenth and the early twenteeth centuries, in which the hot-headed, impatient and reckless younger brother of modern socialism was born – that body of ideas and practices which went down in history under the name of 'communism', having usurped and monopolized that denomination coined in Marx-Engels's 'Communist Manifesto' and supplying it with referents neither intended nor anticipated by its inventors. That new entity was born as a joint offspring of disappointment with the 'laws of history', of frustration caused by the evident lack of progress in the 'maturing' of the proletariat into the role of a revolutionary force, and the growing suspicion that time 'was not on socialism's side': that if it were left to its present management, the flow of time was likely to make the prospect of the socialist transformation yet more distant and doubtful, rather than bringing it nearer and rendering it inevitable.

Sluggish history must be given a powerful boost, the somnolent masses a hefty spur; an awareness of historical necessity must be brought from the outside into the proletarian homes where it was unlikely to be conceived and born. Revolution, unlikely as it was to be initiated *by* 'the masses', needed to be accomplished *for* the 'masses' by revolutionary specialists – 'professional revolutionaries' – who would deploy the state's power of coercion, once they had taken it over, to convert the 'mass' into a genuine revolutionary force – and goad (educate, harangue, prod or if necessary coerce) them into the historical role they were so reluctant (or incapacitated, or just too ignorant) to assume. That could be done even before the capitalist-led industrialization had managed to lift the premodern exploited masses to the status of the working class. Once the professional revolutionaries were trained and drilled into a revolutionary party armed with a knowledge of the 'laws of history' and cemented by iron discipline, the capitalist interlude – the 'site clearing' and 'pump priming' exercise led by capital in the premodern, peasant lands on the fringes of the 'developed world', as in the tsarist Russia – could be skipped and omitted. The entire road to the ideal, orderly, conflict-free and contingency-proof society could be taken, straight from the very beginning and all the way to the finishing line, following the knowledge of 'historical inevitability' and under the supervision, surveillance and command of the bearers of that knowledge. In a nutshell, communism, Lenin's version of socialism, was an ideology and practice of shortcuts – whatever the cost . . .

Put into practice, that idea (much like the strategy deployed to fulfil it) proved to be what Rosa Luxemburg, in her dispute with Lenin, expected it to be: a recipe for serfdom. Even Rosa, however, could not quite imagine the full scale of the atrocity, violence, cruelty, inhumanity and goriness of the exercise and the volume of the resulting human suffering. Pushed to an extreme never tried anywhere else, the modern promise of bliss guaranteed by a rationally designed and rationally run, orderly society was revealed to be a death sentence on human freedom. Brought to an extreme never obtained anywhere else, a society treated by its governing bodies in the way gardens are viewed and tackled by gardeners came to focus on an obsessive and in the end compulsive and coercive tracing, spotting, uprooting and extermination of the social equivalents of 'weeds': that is, humans who did not fit the intended order, and who by their sheer presence dimmed the clarity, polluted the cleanliness and ruffled the harmony of the design. As in all gardens, so in the society-turned-into-a-garden, the uninvited humans – who had sown themselves and settled, like weeds, in all sorts of wrong, because unplanned, places, who had played havoc with the rulers' vision of ultimate harmony and who had cast doubt on the mastery of the rulers-turned-gardeners over their creation – were earmarked for destruction. Instead of bringing nearer the promised comforts of a fully transparent, predictable and accident-free, and for those reasons secure, human cohabitation, the war declared on messiness, contingency and impurity never seemed to end; as it went on, it produced its own, ever new casus belli and conjured up ever new 'weeds' yearning to be destroyed – and both in a profusion that showed little or no inclination to decline.

To sum up, the communist experiment put to an extreme and perhaps ultimate and conclusive test the viability of the modern ambition of complete control over the fate and living conditions of human beings – as well as revealing the awesomeness of the human cost of acting on that ambition. Just as the birth of the communist version of modernity was an integral, perhaps even an unavoidable part of the dawn of 'solid modernity', so its implosion and downfall were part and parcel of that solid modernity's decline and demise. The communist regime shared the fate of the solid-modern ambition to replace the inherited social realities with a reality built by design and made to the measure of allegedly calculable, and duly calculated human needs.

The communist alternative was conceived as a better choice because it was quicker and shorter, a track for a cross-country, steeplechase run, with no time wasted, to eliminate uncertainty from the human condition. It was embraced as the surest way to secure the sort of human existence that would conform with the ideal that was visualized, dreamed of and promised to be reached in the incipient 'solid' phase of the modern era. While its claim to be a better way proved to be, to say the least, highly questionable, the principal reason it fell from grace and to ultimate defeat, however, the last nail in its coffin, was a hitherto unanticipated turn of events: the dissipation and vanishing from view, and in the longer run the explicit rejection, of the target by which the degree of success of the whole exercise was to be measured. *The death knell of the communist experiment was sounded by modernity entering its 'liquid' phase.*

The direct confrontation and competition of the communist with the capitalist alternative of modernity made sense as long (but *only* as long!) as the stake of the rivalry, namely the satisfaction of the sum total of human needs believed to be *finite*, steady and calculable, continued to be shared by both competitors. But in the liquid stage of modernity capitalism opted out from that competition: its wager was put instead on the potential *infinity* of human desires, and its efforts have focused since on catering for their infinite growth: on desires desiring more desire, not their satisfaction; on the multiplying instead of the streamlining of opportunities and choices; on letting loose, not 'structuring', the play of probabilities. The task of melting and recasting extant realities has turned, accordingly, from a one-off and once-and-for-all undertaking into a continuous, presumably permanent, human condition – just as the interplay of connecting and disconnecting turned into the permanent existential modality of 'social networking' that replaced 'social structuring'. For the tasks of servicing the liquid modern form of life the whole concept of communist society was, however, ill-prepared and eminently ill-suited, just as the institutions developed to service the order-building preoccupations of 'solid modernity' were singularly unsuitable for servicing modernity's 'liquid' incarnation. The new condition rendered the goals and means inherited from the 'solid' prehistory of liquid modernity antiquated and redundant; more to the point, counterproductive.

The question of how long the competition between the two version of modernity would have continued if both antagonists had remained loyal to the 'solid modern' faith and precepts remains open and perhaps unaswerable. The drabness and greyness of life under a regime that usurped the right and claimed the ability to decree the size and content of human needs (Agnes Heller et al. memorably characterized communism as 'dictatorship over needs',[3] while the Russian satirist Vladimir Voinovich visualized the residents of a future communist Moscow as men and women starting each day by listening to the official announcement of how large or small their needs for that day had been decreed to be[4]) eliminated that regime from the beauty contest against the increasingly colourful and seductive capitalist bazaar more surely than any other misdemeanour or deficiency. With the advent of the liquid phase of modernity the fall of communism became a foregone conclusion.

The fall . . . Does this mean death? An irreversible demise? The ultimate, once-and-for-all closure of a historical episode dying intestate, leaving no offspring and no legacy except a warning against shortcuts, cutting corners, and 'we know better what is good for you' policies? This remains a question, though – as the replacement of 'solid' by 'liquid' modernity, being neither an improvement pure and simple nor an unmixed blessing, may itself prove to be anything but a once-and-for-all shift of history. The atrocities and sufferings that used to pester the bygone 'solid' phase are now, thank God or History, gone. But other atrocities and sufferings, unknown or only vaguely intuited before, have promptly emerged to take their place in the roster of grievances and dissents. To our contemporaries, the new banes may feel every bit as repulsive as the pains suffered by their ancestors – pains all too easy for our contemporaries to belittle, scorn and dismiss as never having been personally experienced by them. It also needs to be observed that (to borrow Jürgen Habermas's phrase) the 'programme of communism' has remained thus far unfulfilled. Most of the offputting and revolting, immoral aspects of the human condition that made that programme so attractive in the eyes of millions of denizens of 'solid modernity' (such as a blatantly unjust distribution of wealth, widespread poverty, hunger, humiliation and denial of human dignity) are still as much with us, if not even more blatantly, as they were two hundred years ago; if anything, they keep growing in their volume, force, hideousness and loathesomeness.

In India, for instance, that glittering jewel in the liquid modern crown, the country universally looked up to as a most magnificent case of human potential freed and released by the new liquid modern setting, a handful of thriving billionaires coexist with about 250 million people forced to live on less than 1 dollar a day; 42.5 per cent of children under five suffer from malnutrition; 8 million of them suffer acute, severe, continuous and incapacitating hunger, leaving them physically and mentally stunted; 2 million of them die every year for that reason.[5] But poverty, together with humiliation and prospectlessness, its dedicated fellow-travellers, not only persists in countries that have known poverty, misery and malnutrition since time immemorial; it is again visiting lands from which it seemed to have been chased away and banished once and for all with no right of return. In Britain, for instance, 14,000 more children in 2009 than a year before were entitled to free school meals in an attempt to mitigate the outcome of poverty-caused malnutrition. Since Tony Blair's third election victory, the poorest 10 per cent of households have found their incomes falling by £9 a week, while the richest 10 per cent have on average enjoyed a £45 a week increase.[6] And what is at stake in the case of inequality is much more than just hunger and the dearth of food – however much pain they may visit on their victims.

And today we know still more about the multifarious destructive consequences of human inequality than the people knew who grew impatient with the inanities of capitalist mismanagement and joined communist parties in order to speed up their repair. We know, for instance, that in the most unequal societies on the planet, like the United States or Britain, the incidence of mental illness is three times higher than at the bottom of the inequality league; they also rank high in their prison populations, the bane of obesity, teenage pregnancies and (for all their summary wealth!) in death rates for *all* social classes, including the richest strata. Whereas the general level of health is as a rule higher in wealthier countries, among countries of equal wealth death rates fall when the degree of social equality goes up . . . A truly striking finding is that the rising levels of specifically health-related expenditure has had almost no impact on average life expectancy – but a rising level of inequality does have such an impact, and a strongly negative one.

The list of acknowledged 'social ills' tormenting the so-called 'developed societies' is long, and despite all genuine or putative efforts to the contrary is growing longer. In addition to the afflictions already mentioned, it contains items like homicide, infant mortality, rising levels of mental and emotional problems, and a dwindling and waning of the supplies of mutual trust without which social cohesion and cooperation are inconceivable. In each case the scores get less alarming as we move from more to less unequal societies; sometimes the differences between high-inequality and low-inequality societies are truly staggering. The United States is at the top of the inequality league, Japan at the very bottom. In the US almost 500 people per 100,000 are in jail, in Japan fewer than 50. In the US one-third of the population suffers from obesity, in Japan less than 10 per cent. In the US, per thousand women aged 15–16, more than 50 are pregnant; in Japan, just three. In the US, more than a quarter of the population suffer from mental illnesses; in Japan, around 7 per cent. In Japan, Spain, Italy and Germany, societies with a relatively more equal distribution of wealth, one in ten persons reports a mental health problem – as against one in five in more unequal countries like Britain, Australia, New Zealand or Canada.

These are all statistics: sums, averages, and their correlations. Of the causal connections behind those correlations, they say little. But they prod the imagination. And sound an alert. They appeal to the conscience *as well as* to survival instincts. They challenge our all-too-common ethical apathy and moral indifference; but they also show, and beyond reasonable doubt, that the idea of the pursuit of a good life and happiness being a self-referential business for each individual to pursue and perform on his or her own is an idea that is grossly misconceived. That the hope that one can 'do it alone' is a fatal mistake which defies the purpose of self-concern and self-care. We can't get nearer to that purpose while distancing ourselves from other people's misfortunes.

There are powerful reasons to celebrate the anniversary of communism's fall. Yet there are also powerful reasons to pause, and think, and think again, about what happened to the child when the bathwater was poured out of the tub . . . That child is crying; it is crying for our attention.

3

The fate of social inequality in liquid modern times

In 1963–4 Michel Crozier published (first in French and then in English) *The Bureaucratic Phenomenon*, the result of his thorough study of the inner life of large business organizations.[1] Ostensibly, its focus was on the applicability of Max Weber's 'ideal type of bureaucracy', at that time the unquestionable paradigm of all organizational studies. Crozier's principal finding, however, was the presence of not one, but many and different national 'bureaucratic cultures', each profoundly influenced by social and cultural peculiarities of its country. Crozier charged Weber with neglecting these cultural idiosyncrasies which seriously limited the universality of his model. I would, however, suggest that however pioneering might have been his emphasis on culture-bound peculiarities, Crozier's fully and truly epochal discovery was made in the course of disclosing and codifying the strategies deployed by the incumbents of bureaucratic offices, which Crozier charged with departing from Weber's theoretical model and undermining its validity.

Crozier's was, so to speak, an 'immanent' critique of Weber, conducted in the shadow of Weber's vision and from Weber's perspective: it tacitly accepted Weber's presumption that bureaucracy was the foremost embodiment of the modern idea of 'legal-rational' action, and that 'rationalization' was the sole purpose of modern bureaucracy. It also accepted Weber's postulate that it was precisely that purpose, and only that purpose, that could and should provide the key to the logic of bureaucratic practices and its requisites. In his ideal type, Weber portrayed modern bureaucracy as a sort of 'factory of rational conduct', understood as conduct guided by the search for the best means to already given goals. If the objective of the bureaucratic organization was the task it was commanded and entrusted to perform, then its structure and procedures could be explained by the role they played and were designed to play in finding, spelling out and following to the letter the 'most rational' methods of fulfilling that task, that is, the ones that were the most efficient, the least costly, and the best suited to minimizing the risk of error – and to neutralizing or downright eliminating any other, heterogeneous and heteronomic interests, motives and loyalties of its officers that might compete and interfere with that role. But as Crozier found out, the sample of French bureaucratic organizations he studied looked in practice more like 'factories of *irrational* behaviour' – the meaning of 'irrationality' being in this case a derivative-by-refutation of Weber's understanding of 'rationality'. In terms of Weber's admittedly abstract yet allegedly faithful model, the practice of bureaucracy in the French organizations was found by Crozier to generate a lot of 'dysfunction': again a concept dependent on Weber's agenda, in so far as it was explicated as a set of factors inimical to the Weberian version of 'rational behaviour', that is to the unquestionable primacy of goal fulfilment over all other considerations. What Crozier discovered was that instead of concentrating time and energy on the fulfilment of the declared task, the office staff spent a lot of its time and energy on activities irrelevant to that task, or on undertakings that obstructed its fulfilment, or even rendered its implementation impossible. The major dysfunction he discovered and amply recorded was the intergroup struggle for power, influence and privilege.

Such an internal power struggle was endemic in the organizations Crozier studied: each category of functionaries sought more power for itself and tried to secure it by playing the formal rules to their advantage, using loopholes in the statute books or resorting to altogether informal expedients, unlisted among or even explicitly prohibited by the organizational rules. While trying to explain a specifically French, culture-bound departure from the ideal model of the compulsively, obsessively 'rationalizing' vocation and practice of modern bureaucracy, Crozier in my view – as if following William Blake's call 'to see the universe in a grain of sand' – discovered and documented the universal strategy of *all and any power struggle*, the process by which inequality of power – that, so to speak, 'mother of all inequality' – is generated and institutionalized.

That strategy, as I learned then from Crozier, consists at all times and in all places in the *manipulation of insecurity*. Uncertainty, insecurity's principal cause, is by far the most decisive tool of power – indeed, its very substance. As Crozier himself put it, whoever is 'close to the sources of uncertainty' rules. This is so because whoever is cast on the receiving end of uncertainty (more to the point, whoever is confronted with an adversary whose moves cannot be predicted and defy expectations) is disabled and disarmed in their efforts to resist and fight back against discrimination. Groups or categories with limited options or no options to choose from, forced for that reason to follow a monotonous and utterly predictable routine, stand no chance in their power struggle with protagonists who are mobile, free to choose, lavishly supplied with options, and so essentially unpredictable. It is flexible against fixed combat: *flexible* groups, those with many options to choose from, are a constant source of a disabling uncertainty, and so an overwhelming sense of insecurity, for those fixed in a routine – while the flexible don't need to count possible moves and responses by the *fixed* among the risks to their own position and its prospects.

Inside an organization, one category of functionaries therefore strives to force upon the category it wishes to subordinate a maximally detailed and comprehensive code of behaviour, intended ideally to make the conduct of the groups it thereby 'fixes' monotonously regular and so utterly predictable; while it strives to keep its own hands (and legs . . .) untied, so that its moves are impossible to anticipate and go on defying the calculations and predictions of the category earmarked for subordination. Remembering that the idea of 'structuring' stands for the manipulation of probabilities (that is, for making some events highly probable while reducing the probability of some others), we may say that in a nutshell *the foremost strategy of all and any power struggle consists in structuring the counterpart's condition while 'unstructuring', that is deregulating, one's own.* What the adversaries in the power struggle are after is to leave their current or prospective subordinates with no choice but to meekly accept the routine which their current or prospective superiors have set or intend to impose. And if they indeed accept that routine, their behaviour becomes a 'constant', a risk-free variable, no longer a source of uncertainty, and so of no importance to their superiors in calculating their own moves.

There are of course 'natural' limits to the freedom of choice enjoyed by even the freest among the power-holding and power-seeking groups – limits imposed by the social/economic setting in which they operate and by the substance of their operation; limits that remain immune to even the most ingenious and clever stratagems and so practically unencroachable. And the settings in which the power struggle is waged have undergone a truly drastic, radical transformation with the passage from the early 'solid' to the present-day 'liquid' phase of the modern era.

When he was buttonholed by journalists questioning him about the motives behind his sudden decision to defy the most common business practices of the day by doubling the wages of his workers, Henry Ford famously quipped that he did it to enable his workers to buy the automobiles he was selling. In fact, however, his decision was prompted by a much more realistic and indeed rational consideration: while his workers depended on him for their livelihood, Ford in turn depended on them, the locally available labour, the only operators he could use to keep the conveyor belt running, for his wealth and power. The dependence was *mutual*. Because of the bulkiness and fixity of his kind of wealth and power, Ford had little choice but to keep his already tamed and disciplined labour force inside his factory, rather than let them be enticed by better offers from his competitors. Unlike his descendants a century later, Henry Ford Sr was denied the ultimate 'insecurity weapon', the choice of moving his wealth to other places – places teeming with people ready to suffer without a murmur any factory regime, however cruel, in exchange for any living wage, however miserable: just like his labour force, Ford's capital was 'fixed' to the place: it was sunk in heavy and bulky machinery and locked inside tall factory walls. That the dependence was for those reasons mutual, and that the two sides were therefore bound to stay together for a very long time to come, was a public secret of which both sides were acutely aware.

Confronted with such tight interdependence with such a long life expectancy, both sides had to come to the conclusion sooner or later that it was in their interest to elaborate, negotiate and observe a modus vivendi – that is, a mode of coexistence which would include voluntary acceptance of unavoidable limits to their own freedom of manoeuvre and to how far the other side in the conflict of interests could and should be pushed. The sole alternative open to Henry Ford and the swelling ranks of his admirers, followers and imitators would be tantamount to cutting off the branch on which they were willy-nilly perched, to which they were tied just as their labourers were to their workbenches, and from which they could not move to more comfortable and inviting places. Transgressing the limits set by interdependence would mean destroying the sources of their own enrichment; or fast exhausting the fertility of the soil in which their riches had grown and were expected to go on growing, year in year out, in the future – perhaps forever. To put it in a nutshell, there were limits to the inequality which capital could survive. *Both sides of the conflict had vested interests in preventing inequality from running out of control.*

There were, in other words, 'natural' limits to inequality; the main reasons why Karl Marx's prophecy of the 'proletariat's absolute pauperization' became self-refuting, and the main reasons why the introduction of the social state, a state taking care to keep labour in a condition of readiness for employment, became a non-partisan issue, a 'beyond left and right'. They were also the reasons why the state needed to protect the capitalist order against the suicidal consequences of allowing the capitalists' morbid predilections – their rapacity and quest for a fast profit – to go unbridled; and why the state acted on that need by introducing minimum wages or time limits to the working day and week, as well as by the legal protection of labour unions and other weapons of workers' self-defence. And these were the reasons why the widening of the gap separating rich and poor was halted, or even, as one would say today deploying the current idiom, 'turned negative'. To survive, inequality needed to invent the art of self-limitation. And it did, and practised it, even if in fits and starts, for more than a century. All in all, those factors contributed to at least a partial reversal of the trend, to a mitigation of the degree of uncertainty haunting the subordinate classes and thereby to a relative levelling up of the strengthes and chances of the sides engaged in the uncertainty game.

These were the 'macro-social' factors deciding the extent and developmental tendencies of the modern edition of inequality and the prospects of the war waged against it. They were complemented with the micro-social factors already mentioned, operative inside each one of the single-factory battlefields on which the war against inequality was fought. On both levels, however, uncertainty remained the principal weapon of the power struggle, and the manipulation of uncertainties was that struggle's paramount strategy.

In the late 1930s, in a book aptly named *The Managerial Revolution,* James Burnham suggested that managers, hired originally by the owners of the machines and briefed to drill, discipline and supervise their machine operators and to elicit a maximum effort from the labour force, had taken the real power away from their employers – while the owners had gradually turned into stockholders. Managers had been hired and paid for their services, because day-to-day supervision of sloppy and essentially unwilling and resentful labourers was an awkward and cumbersome task, a chore which the owners of industrial plants and their machinery did not relish doing themselves and willingly paid generously to rid themselves of. No wonder the owners used their wealth to buy services they hoped would release them from such an unrewarding and unwanted burden. As it transpired, however, the function of 'managing' – that is, of forcing or cajoling other people to placidly follow a dull and stupefying routine and to do, day in day out, something they would rather not do (recycling managerial coercion into labourers' willingness, the necessities foisted on them into character traits) – was the real power, the power that ultimately counted. The hired managers turned into genuine bosses. Power was now in the hands of those who managed 'productive relations', that is other people's actions, rather than those who owned the 'means of production'. Managers turned the true power-holders, a turn of events which Karl Marx, in his vision of the imminent confrontation between capital and labour, did not anticipate.

In its original sense, as it was bequeathed by the times when the ideal of the industrial process was conceived after the pattern of a homeostatic machine going through predesigned and strictly repetitive motions and kept on a steady, immutable course, managing was indeed a chore. It required meticulous regimentation and close and continuous Panopticon-style surveillance. It needed the imposition of a monotonous routine, bound to stultify the creative impulses of *both* the managed and their managers. It generated boredom and a constantly seething resentment threatening to self-combust into open conflict. It was also a costly way of 'getting things done': instead of enlisting the non-regimented potential of hired labour in the service of the job, it used precious resources to stifle them and keep them out of mischief. All in all, day-to-day management was not the kind of task which resourceful people, people in power, were likely to relish and cherish: they would not perform it a moment longer than they had to, and given the power resources at their disposal they could not be expected to put off that moment for too long. And they did not.

The current 'Great Transformation Mark Two' (to borrow Karl Polanyi's memorable phrase), the emergence of the widely lauded and welcomed 'experience economy' drawing on the totality of the resources of people's personality, warts and all, signals that this moment of 'emancipation of the managers from the burden of managing' has arrived. Using James Burnham's terms, one could describe it as the 'Managerial Revolution Mark Two'; though, as revolutions go, there was little or no change of the incumbents of the office of power. What has happened – what is happening – is more a coup d'état than a revolution: a proclamation from the top that the old game is abandoned and new rules of the game are in force. People who initiated and saw through the revolution remained at the helm – and, if anything, settled in their offices yet more securely than before. This revolution was started and conducted in the name of adding to their power, of further strengthening their grip, and of immunizing their domination against the resentment and rebellion which the form of their domination once generated, before the revolution. Since the second managerial revolution, the power of the managers has been reinforced and made well-nigh invulnerable, by cutting through most of its restraining and otherwise inconvenient strings.

During that second revolution, the managers banished the pursuit of routine and invited the forces of spontaneity to occupy the now vacant supervisors' rooms. They refused to manage; instead, they demanded from the residents, on the threat of eviction, self-management. The right to extend their residential lease was subjected to recurrent competition: after each round, the most playful and the best performing would win the next term of lease, though it was not a guarantee, or even an increased likelihood, that they would emerge unscathed from the next test. On the walls of the banqueting suite of the 'experience economy', the reminder that 'you are as good as your *last* success' (but not as your last but one) replaced the inscription of 'Mene, Tekel, Upharsin' ('counted, weighed, allocated'). Favouring subjectivity, playfulness and performativity, the organizations of the 'experience economy' era had to, wished to, and did prohibit long-term planning and the accumulation of merits. This may indeed keep the residents constantly on the move and busy – in the feverish search of ever new evidence that they are still welcome.

Nigel Thrift, a most insightful analyst of contemporary business elites, has noticed a remarkable change of vocabulary and cognitive frame that marks the new captains of industry, trade and finance, and particularly the most successful among them, the people who 'call the tune' and set the pattern of conduct for lesser or still aspiring members to emulate.[2] To convey the rules of their strategies and the logic of their actions, contemporary business leaders no longer speak of 'engineering' (a notion implying a divide or juxtaposition between those who 'engineer' and that which is 'engineered'), as their grandfathers and even their fathers did, but of 'cultures' and 'networks', 'teams' and 'coalitions' – and of 'influences' rather than of control, leadership or, for that matter, management. In opposition to the now abandoned or shunned concepts, all these new terms convey the message of volatility, fluidity, flexibility, short lifespan. People who deploy such terms are after loosely patched together aggregates (alliances, cooperations, cohabitations, ad hoc teams) that can be assembled, dismantled and reassembled as shifting circumstances require: at short notice or without notice. It is the kind of fluid setting of action that best fits their perception of the surrounding world as 'multiple, complex, and fast moving, and therefore "ambiguous", "fuzzy", and "plastic", uncertain, paradoxical, even chaotic'. Today's business organizations (if one may still be permitted to use that name, an increasingly 'zombie term', as Ulrich Beck would say) tend to have a considerable element of *dis*organization deliberately built into them. The less solid and more readily alterable they are, the better.

Managers shun the 'managerial science' that suggests permanent and stable rules of conduct. Like everything else in such a liquid world, all wisdom and know-how is bound to age quickly, and quickly suck dry and use up the advantages it once offered; so there is a refusal to accept established knowledge, an unwillingness to go by precedents, and a gnawing suspicion as to the value of the received lore of experience in the search for effectiveness and productivity. Managers would rather 'scan the network of possibilities', free to pause for a while whenever opportunity seems to be knocking at their door, and free to move again once opportunity starts knocking elsewhere. They are eager to play the uncertainty game; they seek *chaos* rather than *order*. To volatile and adventurous spirits, as much as to strong and resourceful bodies, chaos promises more chances and more joy. So what they want to hear from their counsellors is how to recycle and rehabilitate the resources previously consigned to rubbish heaps: namely, how to redevelop previously neglected and written off skills (like their emotional impulses, once dismissed as 'irrational'), and unravel inner capacities once suppressed – and now sorely missed by those condemned to swim in turbulent waters.

One can explain the phenomenon of managers retreating from their ancient love affair with order, routine, routine order and orderly routine, and falling in love with chaos and chronic uncertainty instead, as a prudent (or 'rational') adjustment to the conditions of the kind of globalization currently practised, remarkable for devaluing the defensive potential of space by ignoring all and any Maginot lines and dismantling all and any Berlin Walls that were once hoped to protect the oases of order against the invasion of uncertainty. Or one can insist instead that the current revolution in managerial philosophy is itself the prime cause, rather than an effect, of such globalization.

Instead of joining that unpromising priority debate between chicken and egg, I would prefer to suggest that the new global setting and the new patterns of behaviour are closely related to each other, and by now have become each other's necessary complements; and that, as a result, the institutional barriers capable of stopping short the forces promoting inequality from breaking the 'natural' limits to inequality, with all its disastrous, indeed suicidal consequences, are no longer in place, at least at the moment. Even if they haven't as yet been dismantled, the barriers erected for that purpose in the past have proved singularly inadequate to the new task. At the time when they were designed, they were not meant for confronting the present-day volume of uncertainty, fed from apparently inexhaustibly prolific global sources that are no easier to tame with the available political instruments than the fountain of crude oil contaminating the Gulf of Mexico and its surroundings was with the hitherto available technology.

In a nutshell, the new managerial philosophy is that of comprehensive *deregulation*: dismembering the firm and fixed procedural patterns that modern bureaucracy sought to impose. It favours kaleidoscopes over maps, and pointillist time over the linear. It puts intuition, impulse and spurs of the moment over long-term planning and meticulous design. Practices illuminated and inspired by such philosophy result in transforming the uncertainty once viewed as a temporary and transitory irritant – bound to be chased away sooner rather than later from the human condition – into that condition's ubiquitous, intractable and irremovable attribute, sought after and publicly welcome indeed, if not in the open. As a result, the odds in favour of those 'close to the sources of uncertainty', and against those others fixed at uncertainty's receiving end, have been radically multiplied. It is the efforts to narrow the hiatus, to mitigate the polarization of chances and the resulting discrimination that have now been made marginal and transient: they have become spectacularly ineffective, indeed impotent, in stopping the runaway rise of fortune and misery at the two poles of the present-day power axis. They are afflicted by a chronic deficit of power to act and get things done, while power continues to be amassed and stocked by the forces pressing in the opposite direction. State governments seek in vain for local remedies for the globally fabricated deprivations and miseries – just as individuals-by-decree-of-fate (read, by the impact of deregulation) seek in vain for individual solutions to the socially fabricated problems of life.

'The inequality between the world's individuals is staggering,' says Branko Milanovic, the top economist in the research department of the World Bank. 'At the turn of the twenty-first century, the richest 5 per cent of people receive one-third of total global income, as much as the poorest 80 per cent.' While a few poor countries are catching up with the rich world, the differences between the richest and poorest individuals around the globe are huge and likely to be growing. In the words of the 2005 United Nations report on world inequality, 'it would be impossible for the 2.8 billion people living on less than $2 a day to ever match the consumption levels of the rich'. It says that, despite the considerable economic growth in some regions, planetary inequality has grown in the last ten years and the 'wealthy nations are the main beneficiaries of economic development'. Under conditions of a planetary deregulation of capital movements, economic growth does not translate into the growth of equality. Quite the opposite: it is a major factor in enriching the rich and further impoverishing the poor.

In 2008, Glenn Firebaugh pointed out that 'we have a reversal of a longstanding trend, from rising inequality across nations and constant or declining inequality within nations, to declining inequality across nations and rising inequality within them. That's the message of my 2003 book *The New Geography of Global Income Inequality*' – a message since then confirmed.[3] Firebaugh's findings chime well with the framework sketched here for grasping and explaining the contemporary trends and prospects of social inequality. We can only repeat after Crozier that 'those at the source of uncertainty rule', and of course draw profuse gains from their uncontested rule. Capital, free-floating in the 'politics free' global 'space of flows' (as Manuel Castells aptly and famously called it), is keen to search for areas of the globe with low living standards and which are amenable to the 'virgin land' treatment – cashing in on the (temporary and self-destructive) profit-generating differential between the lands with low wages and without institutions of self-defence and state protection of the poor, and the long-exploited lands afflicted by the impact of the 'law of diminishing returns'. The immediate consequence of that 'free floating' of capital emancipated from political control will most probably lead to a shrinking of that differential which set in motion the current tendency of an interstate 'levelling up' of living standards. The countries that released capital into the 'space of flows' find themselves, however, in a situation in which they themselves turn into the objects of uncertainties generated by global finance, and in which their ability to act falls victim to the new power deficit – obliging them, in the absence of global regulation, to retreat step by step from the protection which, in the times preceding the divorce of power from politics and the privatization of uncertainty, they used to promise (and most of the time deliver) to their own native poor.

This could be the explanation for the U-turn of trends noted by Firebaugh. Relieved of their local checks and balances and released into the no-man's land of the global 'politics free' zone, capital accumulated in the 'developed' parts of the world are free to recreate in distant places the conditions that ruled in their countries of origin in the times of 'primitive accumulation'; with a proviso, however, that this time round the bosses are 'absentee landlords', thousands of miles away from the labour they hire. The bosses have unilaterally broken the mutuality of dependence while freely multiplying the numbers of those exposed to the consequences of the bosses' own new freedoms, and even more the number of those who crave to be so exposed . . .

This in its turn cannot but rebound on the conditions of the metropolitan labour left behind by capital's secession: that labour is now constrained not only by the added uncertainty caused by the vastly expanded range of options open to their bosses, but also by the awesomely low prices of labour in the countries where capital in its freedom to move, chooses to temporarily settle. As a result, as Firebaugh observed, the distance between 'developed' and 'poor' countries tends to shrink, whereas in the countries that seemed not long since to have got rid of jarring social inequalities once and for all, the sky's-no-limit growth of the distance between the 'haves' and the 'have nots', known in the Europe of the early nineteenth century, is coming back with vengeance.

4

Strangers are dangers . . .
Are they indeed?

Human uncertainty and vulnerability are the foundations of all political power: it is against those twin, hotly resented yet constant accompaniments of the human condition, and against the fear and anxiety they tend to generate, that the modern state has promised to protect its subjects; and it is mostly from that promise that it has drawn its raison d'être as well as its citizens' obedience and electoral support.

In a 'normal' modern society, vulnerability and insecurity of existence, and the necessity to live and act under conditions of acute and unredeemable uncertainty, are assured by the exposure of life pursuits to notoriously capricious and endemically unpredictable market forces. Except for the task of creating and protecting the legal conditions of market freedoms, political power has no need to contribute to the production of uncertainty and the resulting state of existential insecurity; the vagaries of the market are sufficient to erode the foundations of existential security and keep the spectre of social degradation, humiliation and exclusion hanging over most of society's members. In demanding the subjects' obedience and observance of law, the state may therefore rest its legitimacy on the promise to *mitigate* the extent of the already existing vulnerability and frailty of its citizens' condition: to *limit* harms and damages perpetrated by the free play of market forces, to *shield* the vulnerable against excessively painful blows and to insure the uncertain against the risks that free competition necessarily entails. Such legitimation found its ultimate expression in the self-definition of the modern form of governance as an *État providence*: a community taking upon itself, for its own administration and management, the obligation and promise once imputed to divine providence: to protect the faithful against the inclement vicissitudes of fate, to help them in the event of personal misfortunes and to give them succour in their sorrows.

That formula of political power, its mission, task and function, are all presently receding into the past. Institutions of the 'providential state' are progressively cut down in size, dismantled or phased out, while the restraints previously imposed on business activities and on the free play of market competition and its consequences are removed. The protective functions of the state are tapered and 'targeted', to embrace a small minority of the unemployable and the invalid, though even that minority tends to be reclassified step by step from an object of social care into an issue of law and order; the incapacity of an individual to engage in the market game according to its statutory rules while using their own resources and at their own personal risk tends to be increasingly criminalized or suspected of criminal intention, or at any rate criminal potential. The state washes its hands of the vulnerability and uncertainty arising from the logic (more precisely, the absence of logic) of free markets. The noxious frailty of social status is now redefined as a private affair, a matter for individuals to deal with and cope using the resources in their private possession. As Ulrich Beck put it, individuals are now expected to seek biographical solutions to systemic contradictions.[1]

These new trends have a side-effect: they sap the foundations on which state power, claiming a crucial role in fighting back against and sweeping away the vulnerability and uncertainty haunting its subjects, increasingly rested through the greater part of the modern era. The widely noted growth of political apathy, loss of political interest and commitments ('no more salvation by society', as Peter Drucker succinctly, and famously, phrased it), and a massive retreat by the population from participating in institutionalized politics, both testify to the crumbling of the extant foundations of state power.

Having rescinded its previous programmatic interference with market-produced existential uncertainty and insecurity, and having on the contrary proclaimed that the removal, one by one, of the residual constraints imposed on profit-oriented activities was the prime task of any political power that cares for the well-being of its subjects, the contemporary state must seek other, *non-economic* varieties of vulnerability and uncertainty on which to rest its legitimacy. That alternative seems to have been recently located (first and most spectacularly, but by no means exclusively, by the recent US administration) in the issue of *personal safety*: current or portending, overt or hidden, genuine or putative fears of the *threats to human bodies, possessions and habitats* – whether arising from pandemics and unhealthy diets or lifestyle regimes, or from criminal activities, anti-social conduct by the 'underclass', or most recently global terrorism.

Unlike the existential insecurity born of the market, which is if anything all too genuine, profuse, visible and obvious for comfort, that *alternative* insecurity with which the state hopes to restore its lost monopoly on the chances of redemption must be artificially beefed up, or at least highly dramatized to inspire a sufficient volume of fears, and at the same time outweigh, over-shadow and relegate to a secondary position the *economically generated* insecurity about which the state administration can do next to nothing, nothing being what it is particularly eager to do. Unlike in the case of the market-generated threats to livelihood and welfare, the gravity and extent of the dangers to personal safety must be presented in the darkest of colours, so that the non-materialization of the advertised threats and the predicted blows and sufferings (indeed, anything less than predicted disasters) can be applauded as a great victory of governmental reason over hostile fate: as a result of the laudable vigilance, care and good will of state organs.

In France, the Chirac versus Jospin presidential duel of 2002 degenerated as early as in its preliminary stages into a public auction in which both competitors vied for electoral support by offering ever harsher measures against criminals and immigrants, but above all against immigrants who breed crime and the criminality bred by immigrants.[2] First of all, though, they did their best to refocus the electors' anxiety stemming from the ambient sense of *precarité* (the infuriating insecurity of social position inter-twined with acute uncertainty about the future of their livelihoods) onto fear for personal safety (integrity of the body, personal possessions, home, neighbourhood). On 14 July 2001 Chirac set the infernal machine in motion, announcing the need to fight 'that growing threat to safety, that rising flood' in view of an almost 10 per cent increase in delinquency in the first half of the year (also announced on that occasion) and declaring that a 'zero tolerance' policy was bound to become law once he was re-elected. The tune of the presidential campaign had been set, and Jospin was quick to join in, elaborating his own variations on the shared motif (though, unexpectedly to the main soloists, but certainly not to sociologically wise observers, it was the extreme right-wing voice of Le Pen that rose to the top as the purest and so the most audible). On 28 August, Jospin proclaimed 'a battle against insecurity', vowing 'no laxity', while on 6 September Daniel Vaillant and Marylise Lebranchu, his ministers of internal affairs and justice, respectively, swore that they wouldn't show any tolerance of delinquency in any form. Vaillant's immediate reaction to the attacks in the United States on 11 September had been to increase the powers of the police aimed principally against the juveniles of the 'ethnically alien' *banlieues*, the housing estates outside Paris where, according to the official version (the version convenient to the officials), the devilish concoction of uncertainty and insecurity poisoning Frenchmen's lives was brewed. Jospin himself went on castigating and reviling, in ever more vitriolic terms, the 'angelic school' of the softly-softly approach, which he had sworn never to belong to in the past and never join in the future. The auction went on, and the bids climbed skywards. Chirac promised to create a ministry of internal security, to which Jospin responded with a commitment to a ministry 'charged with public security' and the 'coordination of police operations'. When Chirac brandished the idea of locked centres for confining the juvenile delinquents, Jospin echoed the promise with a vision of 'locked structures' for them, outbidding his opponent with the prospect of 'sentencing on the spot'.

No reminder is needed that little if anything has changed since. More than to anything else, Nicolas Sarkozy, Chirac's successor, owed his convincing electoral success to playing on popular fears and the desire for a strong power able to arrest and fight back against the further fears bound to plague the future. He goes on using the same game to chase away from the newspaper headlines the news of the unemployment figures relentlessly rising under his presidency and the relentless fall in the incomes of the majority of

the French. To do that, he resorts to the tested expedient of col-
lapsing the issue of existential security into that of street violence,
and street violence into that of the newcomers from the poor
regions of the planet.

A mere three decades ago, Portugal was (alongside Turkey) the
main supplier of the 'guest workers' the German burghers feared
would despoil their homely townscapes and undercut their social
compact, the foundation of their security and comfort. Today,
thanks to its sharply improved fortunes, Portugal has turned from
a labour-*exporting* into a labour-*importing* country. The hardships
and humiliations suffered while earning bread in foreign countries
have been promptly forgotten, 27 per cent of Portuguese have
declared that neighbourhoods infested with crime and foreigners
are their main worry, and the newcomer politician Paulo Portas,
playing a single, fiercely anti-immigration card, helped a new
right-wing coalition into power (just as Pia Kiersgaard's Danish
People's Party did in Denmark, Umberto Bossi's Northern League
in Italy, the radically anti-immigrant Progress Party in Norway –
and virtually all the mainstream parties in the Netherlands; in
other words, in countries that not so long ago sent their children
to faraway lands to seek the bread their homelands were unable
to offer).

News like this easily makes it to the front page (like the panic-
mongering, xenophobic title aimed at ruffling feathers, 'UK plan
for asylum crackdown', in the *Guardian* of 13 June 2002; no need
to mention the banners on the tabloid front pages . . .). The main
bulk of the planet-wide immigrant phobia stays hidden from
Western Europe's attention (indeed, knowledge), however, and
never makes it to the surface. 'Blaming the immigrants' – the
strangers, the newcomers, and particularly the newcomers among
the strangers – for all aspects of social malaise (and first of all for
the nauseating, disempowering feeling of *Unsicherheit, incertezza,
precarité*, insecurity) is fast becoming a global habit. As Heather
Grabbe, research director for the Centre for European Reform,
put it, 'the Germans blame the Poles, the Poles blame the
Ukrainians, the Ukrainians blame the Kirghiz and Uzbeks',[3] while
countries too poor to attract significant numbers of neighbours
desperately seeking a livelihood, like Romania, Bulgaria, Hungary
or Slovakia, turn their wrath against the usual suspects and stand-
by culprits: local but drifting, shunning fixed addresses, and there-

fore perpetual 'newcomers' and outsiders, always and everywhere – the Gypsies.

A permanent state of alert: dangers proclaimed to be lurking just around the next corner, oozing and leaking from terrorist camps masquerading as Islamic religious schools and congregations, from immigrant-populated *banlieues*, from the underclass-infested mean streets, the 'rough districts' incurably contaminated by violence, the no-go areas of big cities; paedophiles and other sex offenders on the loose, obtrusive beggars, blood-thirsty juvenile gangs, loiterers and stalkers ... Reasons to be afraid are many; since their genuine number and intensity are impossible to calculate from the perspective of narrow personal experience, yet another, perhaps the most powerful reason, to be frightened is added: one does not know where and when the words of warning will turn into flesh.

Contemporary menaces, and particularly the most horrifying among them, are as a rule distantly located, concealed and surreptitious, seldom close enough to be directly witnessed and very rarely accessible to individual scrutiny – for all practical purposes invisible. Most of us would never have learned of their existence were it not thanks to the panics inspired and boosted by the mass media and the alarming prognoses composed by experts and swiftly picked up, endorsed and reinforced by cabinet members and trade companies – hurrying as they do to turn all that excitement into political or commercial profit. As we, 'the ordinary people' occupied with our individual small-scale daily affairs, know of those awesome but faraway dangers only indirectly, it is possible, indeed much too easy, to manipulate our – public – attitudes; to play down or silence the dangers that promise no political or financial gains, while grossly inflating, or even inventing, others, better suited to politically or commercially profitable exploitation. But as Moazzam Begg, a British Muslim arrested in January 2002 and released without charge after three years spent at Baghram and Guantanamo Bay prisons, rightly points out in his book, published in 2006 under the title *Enemy Combatant*, the overall effect of a life lived under virtually incessant security alerts, such as warmongering, justifications of torture, arbitrary imprisonment and terror, is to 'have made the world much worse'.

Whether worse or not, I would also add: not a bit more secure; most certainly, the world today feels considerably less secure than it did a dozen or two dozen years ago. It looks as though the paramount effect of the profuse and immensely costly extraordinary security measures undertaken in the last decade has been a *deepening of our sense of danger, of risk, and of insecurity.* And little in the present tendency promises a speedy return to the comforts of security. Sowing the seeds of fear produces rich crops in politics and trade; and the allure of an opulent harvest inspires seekers of political and commercial gain to break open ever new lands to fear-growing plantations . . .

In principle, security concerns and ethical motivations are at cross-purposes: the prospects of security and the intensity of ethical intentions are at loggerheads.

What casts security and ethics in principled opposition to each other (an opposition excruciatingly difficult to overcome and reconcile) is the contrast between divisiveness and communion: the drive to separate and exclude which is endemic to the first versus the inclusive, unifying tendency constitutive of the second. Security generates an interest in spotting risks and sorting them out for elimination, and for that reason it targets potential sources of danger as objects of 'pre-emptive' exterminating action, unilaterally undertaken. The targets of this action are by the same token excluded from the universe of moral obligation. Targeted individuals and groups or categories of individual are denied human subjectivity and recast as objects pure and simple, located irrevocably at the receiving end of action. They become entities whose sole relevance (the only aspect taken into consideration when their treatment is planned) to those applying the 'security measures' on behalf of those whose security is presumed or declared to be under threat is the threat they already constitute, may constitute, or may credibly be charged with constituting. Denial of subjectivity disqualifies the selected targets as potential partners in dialogue; whatever they might say, and whatever they might have said if given a voice, is a priori declared immaterial, if listened to at all.

The incapacitation of the humanity of the targets of action goes far beyond that passivity ascribed by Emmanuel Levinas, the greatest French ethical philosopher, to the Other as the object of ethical responsibility (according to Levinas, the Other commands me by his *weakness*, not strength; he gives me orders by *refraining* from giving them; it is the unassumingness and the silence of the

Other that trigger my ethical impulse). Using Levinas's vocabulary, we may say that casting others as 'security problems' leads to an effacing of 'face' – a metaphoric name for those aspects of the Other that put us in a condition of ethical responsibility and guide us to ethical action. Incapacitating that face as a potential (unarmed, non-coercive) force evoking or awakening the moral impulse is the hub of what is understood by 'dehumanization'. Inside the 'universe of moral obligations', Moazzam Begg's three-year imprisonment without a crime, and torture administered to squeeze out of him an admission of guilt to (retrospectively) justify it, would be an outrage and an atrocity. Deprived of ethically significant 'face' by the fact of being classified as a security threat and thereby evicted from the universe of moral obligations, Begg was however a legitimate object of 'security measures', declared by the same token to be ethically indifferent or neutral ('adi-aphoric' in my vocabulary) by definition. The extermination of Jews, Gypsies or homosexuals was for its perpetrators a sanitary action (crystals of Zyklon B, originally produced to poison vermin, were sprinkled through the roof of gas chambers by 'sanitary officers'). The Tutsi were summarily described by the Hutu, their murderers, as 'cockroaches'.

Once *stripped* of 'face', the weakness of the Other invites violence naturally and effortlessly, just as when face is *donned* the same weakness lays open an infinite expanse for the ethical capacity of succour and care. As rendered by Jonathan Littell, 'the weak are a threat to the strong, and invite the violence and murder that pitilessly strike them down'.[4] Let's note the *pitilessness* that marked the activity of striking them down – pity being one of the foremost and most salient sensations defining moral stance . . .

Jonathan Littell's attempts to reconstruct the deceptively invit-ing and smooth road that once brought the *masses* of unsuspecting men and women – confused, ingenuous and gullible, frightened by the earthquakes of a great war and the great economic collapse that followed it, and so exceptionally easy to be manipulated and led astray – to the inhuman 'logical limits' of the human craze for security. Begg, on the other hand, reports the fate of only those *selected few* who accidentally and inadvertently fell victim to or became 'collateral casualties' of extreme 'security measures' (people who, as their tormentors retrospectively explained, just 'happened to be in the wrong place at the wrong time'). The point is, though, that the damage done by securitarian passions spreads even wider and reaches deeper than is suggested by the most atrocious and outrageous, and so most publicized, cases, condemned and regretted, extreme and/or 'extraordinary'.

Security obsessions are inexhaustible and insatiable; once they take off and are let loose, there is no stopping them. They are self-propelling and self-exacerbating; as they acquire their own momentum, they need no further boost from outside factors – they produce, on a constantly rising scale, their own reasons, explanations and justifications. The fever kindled and heated by the introduction, entrenchment, servicing and tightening of 'security measures' becomes the sole boost needed by the fears, anxieties and tensions of insecurity and uncertainty to reproduce, grow and proliferate. However radical they already are, stratagems and contraptions designed, obtained and put into operation for the sake of security will hardly prove radical enough to qualm the fears – not for long, at any rate. Each of them may be outwitted, superseded and rendered obsolete by the treacherous plotters who learn how to by-pass or ignore them, thus overcoming every successive obstacle erected in their way.

Whatever happens to cities in their history, one feature remains constant: cities are spaces where strangers stay and move in close proximity to each other. The ubiquitous presence of strangers, constantly within sight and reach, inserts a large dose of perpetual uncertainty into all city dwellers' life pursuits; that presence is a prolific and never resting source of anxiety and of an aggressiveness that is usually dormant but time and again erupts.

Strangers also provide a convenient – handy – outlet for our inborn fear of the unknown, the uncertain and the unpredictable. In chasing strangers away from our homes and streets, the frightening ghost of uncertainty is, if only for a brief moment, exorcised: the horrifying monster of insecurity is burnt in effigy. Despite these exorcisms, our liquid modern life remains stubbornly erratic and capricious, however, and so insecure; relief tends to be short-lived, and the hopes attached to even the toughest of measures are dashed as soon as they are raised.

A stranger is, by definition, an agent moved by intentions which can at best be guessed – but of which we can never be sure. In all the equations we compose when we deliberate on what to do and how to behave, the stranger is an unknown variable. A stranger is, after all, 'strange': a bizarre and puzzling being, whose intentions and reactions may be thoroughly different from those of ordinary (common, familiar) folk. And so, even when strangers do not behave aggressively, or are knowingly and explicitly resented, they are 'subconsciously' discomforting: their sheer presence makes a tall order of the already daunting task of predicting the effects of our actions and their chances of success. And yet the sharing of space with strangers, living in the (as a rule uninvited and unwelcome) proximity of strangers, is a condition that city residents usually find it difficult, and sometimes impossible, to escape.

Since the stubborn proximity of strangers is urban dwellers' non-negotiable fate, some modus vivendi to make cohabitation palatable and life livable *must* be designed, tried out and tested. The way we go about gratifying this need is, however, a matter of *choice*. And choices are made, day in, day out, whether by commission or omission, by design or default. They are made by conscious decision or just through following, blindly and mechanically, the customary patterns of conduct; by wide-ranging reflection and discussion, or just through following trusted, because currently fashionable and widely deployed, means. Opting out from the search for a modus co-vivendi is also one of the possible choices.

Of São Paulo, the largest, most bustling and fast expanding Brazilian city, for instance, Teresa Caldeira writes: 'São Paulo is today a city of walls. Physical barriers have been constructed everywhere – around houses, apartment buildings, parks, squares, office complexes and schools . . . A new aesthetics of security shapes all types of constructions and imposes a new logic of surveillance and distance . . .'[5] Anyone who can afford it buys himself or herself a residence in a 'condominium', intended as a hermitage: physically inside, but socially and spiritually outside the city. 'Closed communities are supposed to be separate worlds. Their advertisements propose a total "way of life" which would represent an alternative to the quality of life offered by the city and its deteriorated public space.' A most prominent feature of the condominium is its 'isolation and distance from the city . . . Isolation means separation from those considered to be socially inferior' and, as the developers and real estate agents insist, 'the key factor to assure this is security. This means fences and walls surrounding the condominium, guards on duty twenty-four hours a day controlling the entrances, and an array of facilities and services for keeping the others out.'

As we all know, fences have to have two sides . . . Fences divide an otherwise continuous space into an 'inside' and an 'outside', but what is the 'inside' for those on one side of the fence is the 'outside' for those on the other. The residents of condominiums fence themselves out of the hurly-burly and rough life of the city in an oasis of calm and safety. By the same token, though, they fence all the others out of the decent and agreeable, secure places, and into their own, admittedly shabby and squalid streets. The fence separates the 'voluntary ghetto' of the high and mighty from the enforced ghettos of the low and hapless. For the insiders of the voluntary ghetto, the involuntary ghettos are spaces where 'we won't go in'. For the insiders of the involuntary ghettos, the area to which they have been confined is the space where 'we can't get out'.

Paradoxically, originally constructed to provide safety for all their inhabitants, cities are associated more often these days with danger than security. As Nan Elin puts it, the 'fear factor has certainly grown, as indicated by the growth in locked car and house doors and security systems, the popularity of "gated" and "secure" communities for all age and income groups, and the increasing surveillance of public spaces, not to mention the unending reports of danger emitted by the mass media.'[6]

Genuine and putative threats to the body and the property of the individual are fast turning into a major, perhaps the main consideration whenever the merits or disadvantages of a living place are assessed. Threats have also been assigned top position in real-estate marketing policy. Uncertainty about the future, the frailty of social position and *existential insecurity*, those ubiquitous accompaniments of life in the 'liquid modern' world, may have their roots and be gathering force in remote places, yet the anxieties and passions they generate tend to be focused on the nearest targets, and channelled into concerns with *personal safety*: the kind of concerns that condense in turn into segregationist and exclusionist urges, inexorably leading to wars over urban space.

As we can learn from the perceptive study by Steven Flusty, the American architectural and urbanist critic, servicing these wars and, particularly, designing ways to deny adversaries access to the space claimed are the most salient concerns of architectural innovation and urban development in American cities.[7] The most proudly advertised novelties are 'interdictory spaces', 'designed to intercept, repel or filter the would-be users'. Explicitly, the purpose of 'interdictory spaces' is to divide, segregate and exclude – not to build bridges, easy passages and hospitable meeting places; not to facilitate but to break off communication; all in all to separate people, not bring them together. The architectural and urbanist inventions listed and named by Flusty are the technologically updated equivalents of the premodern moats, turrets and embrasures of the city walls; instead of defending the city and all its inhabitants against the enemy outside, they are built to set the city residents apart. Among the inventions named by Flusty there is 'slippery space' – 'space that cannot be reached, due to contorted, protracted, or missing paths of approach'; 'prickly space' – 'space that cannot be comfortably occupied, defended by such details as wall-mounted sprinkler heads activated to clear loiterers or ledges sloped to inhibit sitting'; and 'jittery space' – 'space that cannot be utilised unobserved due to active monitoring by roving patrols and/or remote technologies feeding to security stations'. They all, and others like them, have but one purpose: to cut off extraterritorial enclaves, to erect little fortresses inside which the members of the supraterritorial global elite can groom, cultivate and relish their bodily independence and spiritual isolation from locality.

The developments described by Steven Flusty are high-tech manifestations of the ubiquitous mixophobia, a widespread reaction to the mind-boggling, spine-chilling and nerve-wracking variegation of human types and lifestyles rubbing shoulders in the streets of contemporary cities and in their 'ordinary' (read, unprotected by 'interdictory spaces') living districts. Releasing segregationist urges may relieve the rising tension. Confusing and disconcerting differences can be unassailable and intractable – but perhaps the toxin can be squeezed out of their fangs by assigning to each form of life its separate, isolated, well-marked and, above all, well-guarded physical space. Perhaps one can secure for oneself, for one's kith and kin and other 'people like myself', a territory free from that jumble and mess that irredeemably poisons other areas of the city.

'Mixophobia' manifests itself in a drive towards islands of similarity and sameness amidst the sea of variety and difference. The reasons for mixophobia are banal – easy to understand, if not necessarily easy to forgive. As Richard Sennett suggests, 'the "we" feeling, which expresses a desire to be similar, is a way for men to avoid the necessity of looking deeper into each other'. It thereby promises some spiritual comfort: the prospect of making togetherness easier by making redundant the effort to understand, negotiate and compromise. 'Innate to the process of forming a coherent image of community is the desire to avoid actual participation. Feeling common bonds without common experience occurs in the first place because men are afraid of participation, afraid of the dangers and the challenges of it, afraid of its pain.'[8] The drive towards a 'community of similarity' is a sign of withdrawal not just from the otherness *outside*, but also from a commitment to the lively yet turbulent, engaged yet cumbersome interaction *inside*.

Choosing the escape option prompted by mixophobia has an insidious and deleterious consequence of its own: the more consistently deployed, self-perpetuating and self-reinforcing the strategy is, the more ineffective it is. The longer people spend in the company of others 'like them', with whom they 'socialize' perfunctorily and matter-of-factly with no risk of miscomprehension, hardly ever coming across the onerous need to translate between distinct universes of meaning, the more they are likely to 'de-learn' the art of negotiating meanings and modes of cohabitation. As they fail to learn or forget the skills needed to live with difference, they view the prospect of confronting the strangers face-to-face with rising apprehension. Strangers tend to appear ever more frightening as they become increasingly 'strange' – alien, unfamiliar and incomprehensible – and as the mutual communication which could eventually assimilate their 'otherness' to one's own lifeworld loses substance and fades, or never takes off in the first place. The drive to a homogeneous, territorially isolated environment may be triggered by mixophobia; but practising territorial separation is that mixophobia's lifebelt and food purveyor.

Mixophobia, though, is not the sole combatant on the urban battlefield. City living is a notoriously ambivalent experience. It repels but also attracts, yet it is the same aspects of city life that, intermittently or simultaneously, attract and repel . . . The messy variety of the urban environment is a source of fear, yet the same twinkling and glimmering of urban scenery, never short of novelty and surprise, boasts a charm and seductive power that is difficult to resist.

Confronting the never-ending and constantly dazzling spectacle of the city is not therefore experienced unambiguously as a curse; nor does sheltering from it feel like an unmixed blessing. The city prompts mixo*philia* as much as mixo*phobia*. City life is an intrinsically and irreparably ambivalent affair. The bigger and more heterogeneous a city, the more attractions it can support and offer. A massive concentration of strangers is, simultaneously, a repellent and a most powerful magnet, drawing to the city ever new cohorts of men and women weary of the monotony of rural or small town life, fed up with its repetitive routine and despairing of its dearth of chances. Variety promises many and different opportunities, fitting all skills and any taste. It seems that mixophilia, just like mixophobia, is a self-propelling, self-propagating and self-invigorating tendency. Neither of the two is likely to exhaust itself, nor lose any of its vigour. Mixophobia and mixophilia coexist in every city, but they coexist as well inside every one of the city's residents. Admittedly, this is an uneasy coexistence, full of sound and fury – though signifying a lot to the people on the receiving end of liquid modern ambivalence.

It all started in the United States, but leaked into Europe and has by now spilt across most European countries: the tendency of better-off urban dwellers to buy themselves out of the crowded city streets where everything can happen but where little if anything at all can be predicted – and into 'gated communities': those walled-off developments with strictly selective entry, surrounded by armed guards and stuffed with closed-circuit TV and intruder alarms. Those lucky few who have bought themselves into a closely guarded 'gated community' pay an arm and a leg for 'security services': that is, for the banishment of all mixing. Gated 'communities' are piles of compact private cocoons suspended in a social void.

Inside 'gated communities' the streets are usually empty. And so if someone who 'does not belong', a *stranger*, appears on the pavement, he or she will be promptly spotted – before a prank or any damage can be done. As a matter of fact, anybody you can see walking past your windows or front door can fall into the category of strangers, those frightening people of whom you can't be sure what their intentions are and what they will do next. Everybody might be, unknowingly to you, a prowler or a stalker: an intruder with ill intentions. We live, after all, in the times of mobile telephones (not to mention MySpace, Facebook and Twitter): friends can exchange messages instead of visits, all the people we know are constantly 'online' and able to inform us in advance of their intention to pop in, and so a sudden, unannounced knock on the door or a ringing of the bell is an extraordinary event and so a signal of potential danger. Inside a 'gated community', the streets are kept empty, to render the entry of a stranger, or someone behaving like a stranger, blatant and easy to spot – and therefore too risky to be tried.

The term 'gated *community*' is a misnomer. As we read in a 2003 research report published by the University of Glasgow, there is 'no apparent desire to come into contact with the "community" in the gated and walled area . . . Sense of community is lower in gated "communities".' However the settlers might justify their decision to setttle, they do not pay exorbitant rental or purchase prices in order to find themselves a 'community' – that notoriously intrusive and obtrusive 'collective busybody', opening its arms to you only to hold you down as if in steely forceps. Even if they say (and sometimes believe) otherwise, people pay all that money in order to *liberate* themselves from unwanted company: *to be left alone.* Inside the walls and the gates live loners: people who will only tolerate the 'community' they fancy at the moment, and only at the moment they fancy it . . .

A large majority of researchers agree that the main motive prompting people to lock themselves inside the walls and the CCTV of a 'gated community', whether consciously or subconsciously, explicitly or tacitly, is their desire to keep the wolf from the door, which they translate as keeping strangers at arm's length. Strangers are dangers, and so every stranger is a portent of danger. Or so, at least, they believe. And what they wish more than anything else is to be secure from danger. More exactly, though, to be secure from the daunting, harrowing, incapacitating *fear* of insecurity. They hope that the walls will protect them from that fear.

The snag, however, is that there is more than one reason to feel insecure. Whether credible or fanciful, the rumours of rising crime and of throngs of burglars or sexual predators lying in wait for an occasion to strike produce just one of those reasons. After all, we feel insecure because our jobs, and so our incomes, social standing and dignity, are under threat. We are not insured against the threat of being made redundant, excluded and evicted, losing the position we cherish and believe to have earned as ours forever. The partnerships we cherish are not foolproof and secure either: even in the calmest of moments we may feel subterranean tremors and expect earthquakes. The familiar cosy neighbourhood may be threatened by being run down in order to clear its site for new developments. All in all, it would be downright silly to hope that all those well- or ill-founded anxieties will be placated and put to rest once we've surrounded ourselves with walls, armed guards and CCTV cameras.

But what about that (ostensibly) prime reason to opt for a 'gated community', our fear of physical assault, violence, burglary, car theft and obtrusive beggars? Won't we at least put paid to *that* kind of fear? Alas, even on that front the gains hardly justify the losses. As signalled by the most acute observers of contemporary urban life, the likelihood of being assaulted or robbed may fall once you are behind the gates (though research conducted recently in California, perhaps the main stronghold of the 'gated community' obsession, found no statistically significant difference between gated and non-gated spaces) – the persistence of fear, however, will not. Anna Minton, the author of a thorough study of *Ground Control: Fear and Happiness in the Twenty-First-Century City*, tells the case of Monica, who 'spent the whole night lying awake and far more scared than she had ever been in the twenty years she had lived on an ordinary street' when 'one night the electronically controlled gates went wrong and had to be propped open'. Behind the walls, anxiety grows instead of dissipating – and so does the dependence of the residents' state of mind on 'new and improved' high-tech gadgets, marketed with the promise to put danger, and fear of danger, out of court. The more gadgets one surrounds oneself with, the greater is the fear that some of them may 'go wrong'. And the more time one spends worrying about the menace lurking in every stranger, and the less time one spends in the company of strangers, the further one's 'tolerance and appreciation for the unexpected recedes' and the less one is able to confront, handle, enjoy and appreciate the liveliness, variety and vigour of urban life. Locking oneself in a gated community in order to chase fears away is like draining water out of a pool to make sure that the children learn to swim in complete safety . . .

Oscar Newman, the American town planner and architect, suggested in 1972, in an article and then a book with the tell-all title *Defensible Space: People and Design in the Violent City*,[9] that the preventive medicine against fear of urban violence is a clear marking of boundaries – an act that will discourage strangers from trespassing. The city is violent and teeming with dangers because it is full of strangers: that is what Newman and dozens of his enthusiastic apostles and converts had decided. Want to avert misfortune? Keep strangers at a safe distance. Make the space around brightly lit, easily watchable, easily seen through – and your fears will vanish, you'll savour at long last that wondrous taste of safety. As experience has shown, though, concerns with making space 'defensible' have led to a sharp rise in security concerns. Tokens and symptoms of security 'being a problem' keep reminding us of our insecurities. As Anna Minton put it in her study: 'The paradox of security is that the better it works the less it should be necessary. Yet, instead the need for security can become addictive . . .'[10] Of safety and security, there is never enough. Once you start drawing and fortifying borders, there is no stopping. The principal beneficiary is our fear: it thrives and exuberates as it feeds on our border-drawing and border-arming efforts.

In sharpest conceivable opposition to Newman's opinion stand the recommendations penned by Jane Jacobs: it is precisely in the crowdedness of the city street and the profusion of strangers that we find succour and free ourselves from the fear oozing from the city, that 'great unknown'. The short word for that link, she says, is *trust*. Trust in the comforting safety of city streets is distilled from the multitude of minute sidewalk encounters and contacts. The sediment and lasting trace of casual public contacts is a tissue of togetherness-in-public woven of civil respect and trust. The absence of trust is a disaster to a city street – Jacobs concludes.[11]

Mirosław Bałka, in his 2009 installation commissioned for the Turbine Hall at Tate Modern in London, picks up where Jane

Jacobs left off, achieving in one bold yet simple installation what a long line of scholars had struggled to compose and depict in hundreds of learned and opaque books. The gates to the 30-metre long tunnel-like chamber were wide and invitingly open, signalling a public space. But there was no light at the end of the tunnel which Bałka invited you to explore. Painted pitch-black, the interior could not be darker. 'Dark' is the epitome of that awesome and fearsome unknown lurking in the experience of the city. Dark space is emptiness, the void, the naught incarnate: and you may suspect that it *looks* empty only because your sight is poor, your power to pierce the darkness inadequate, your imagination failing. That sensual emptiness may be just a disguise and a cover-up for most terrifying corporeal contents. You suspect – you *know* – that in a dark space everything may happen, whereas you don't know what to expect, let alone how to deal with it once it happens.

No one would therefore blame you if you hesitated to enter that darkness, were you to find yourself in the Turbine Hall alone. Immersing themselves unaccompanied in that black hole of unexplored wilderness is something only the most reckless among us, or mindless adventurers, would dare to do. But fortunately there are so many people around you, all hurrying to enter! And so many people already inside! Once you join them, you will feel their presence. Not an obtrusive, harrowing presence, but soothing and encouraging . . . A presence of strangers miraculously transformed into fellow humans. A presence emanating confidence, not anxiety. When you are sunk in the void of the great unknown, freezing mind and senses, shared humanity is your lifeboat; the warmth of human togetherness is your salvation. This is at any rate what Mirosław Bałka's oeuvre told and taught me, and for which I am grateful.

The streets of 'defensive spaces' and gated communities need, ideally, to be emptied of strangers, even if the thoughts and efforts invested in the cleansing job prevents you from ever forgetting your fear. The tunnel in the Turbine Hall of Tate Modern is, on the contrary, tightly packed with strangers; but it is also empty of fear – a fear-free area if ever there was one. Miraculously, the darkest of spaces has turned into the fear-freest of zones . . .

I guess that the word 'fear' wouldn't leap to your mind when you reported your experience of the inside of that tunnel. Just possibly, you would talk back home about merriment and relish . . .

To sum up, perhaps the most pernicious, seminal and long-term effect of the security obsession (the 'collateral damage' it perpetrates) is the sapping of mutual trust and the sowing and breeding of mutual suspicion. With lack of trust, borderlines are drawn, and with suspicion, they are fortified with mutual prejudices and recycled into frontlines. The deficit of trust inevitably leads to a wilting of communication; in avoiding communication, and in the absence of interest in its renewal, the 'strangeness' of strangers is bound to deepen and acquire ever darker and more sinister tones, which in turn disqualifies them even more radically as potential partners in dialogue and the negotiation of a mutually safe and agreeable mode of cohabitation. The treatment of strangers as a 'security problem' pure and simple stands behind one of the examples of the veritable 'perpetuum mobile' among patterns of human interaction. The mistrust of strangers, and the tendency to stereotype them all, or selected categories of them, as delayed action bombs bound to explode, grow more intense from their own logic and momentum, needing no further proof of their appropriateness and no additional stimuli from the inimical acts of the targeted adversary (rather they themselves produce such proof and stimuli in profusion). All in all, the major effect of the securitarian obsession is the fast *growth* instead of a shrinking of the mood of insecurity, with all its accoutrements of fear, anxiety, hostility, aggressiveness and a fading or silencing of moral impulses.

All that does not mean that security and ethics are irreconcilable and bound to remain so. It only signals the pitfalls the securitarian obsession is bound to scatter on the road towards the peaceful, mutually profitable and safe cohabitation (and indeed cooperation) of ethnicities, denominations and cultures in our globalized world of diasporas. Alas, although with the sharpening and entrenching of human differences in almost every contemporary human settlement and every neighbourhood, a well-disposed and respectful dialogue between diasporas is becoming an ever more important, indeed crucial, condition of our shared planetary survival, it is also, for the reasons which I have tried to list above, more difficult to attain and defend against present and future forces. Being difficult, however, means only one thing: the need for a lot of good will, dedication, readiness for compromise, mutual respect and a shared distaste for any form of human humiliation; and, of course, a firm determination to restore the lost balance between the value of security and that of ethical propriety. With all these conditions met, and only once they are all met, it is dialogue and agreement (Hans Gadamer's 'fusion of horizons') that might (just might) in their turn become the new 'perpetuum mobile' dominant among the patterns of human cohabitation. That transformation, will have no victims – only beneficiaries.

5

Consumerism and morality

One should beware of pronouncing unambiguous verdicts on the convoluted relationship between consumerism and morality. As things look at the moment, that relationship is no different from the plight of numerous contemporary marriages: the partners find cohabitation rugged and thorny, full of sound and fury, and time and again repellent and unendurable – and yet they can hardly live without each other, their divorce being all but an unthinkable option.

To be sure, in the case of consumerism and morality the relationship is anything but symmetrical. One partner, the consumer market, lavishes on the other, morality, nothing but unqualified praise; like all lovers true to their name, it glorifies the splendours of its beloved, while closing its eyes to its occasional misdemeanours; its public declarations, known under the name of 'advertising copy' or 'commercials', figure among the most rhapsodic and sublime oeuvres of love poetry. It is the other partner, morality, who sniffs out duplicity behind the declarations of unswerving loyalty and dedicated service, as well as malicious and selfish intentions behind the manifestations of concern, care and assistance. That other partner would repeat, taking a leaf from Virgil's Laocoön: *timeo mercatores et dona ferentes* – beware markets even bearing gifts. And yet, however deep its mistrust of the giver, it dares not refuse the gifts. Indeed, what would its own chances of survival be had it decided to spurn them?

Emmanuel Levinas, perhaps the greatest ethical philosopher of our time, can throw some light on the controversial, in many ways baffling and logic-defying interaction between these two both inseparable and unreconcilable partners. If common opinion, the scholarly and the commonsensical alike, sides with the famous Hobbesian verdict on society as a contraption saving humans from the consequences of their own morbid inclinations (which, if unchecked by the coercive powers of society, would make human life 'nasty, brutish and short'), Levinas argues for the indispensability of society in terms of a different role it is called on to play. Unconditional responsibility for the Other, that foundation of all morality, is – so he muses – a demand made to the measure of saints, not of average, ordinary individuals as most of us are. Few people can manage to rise to the level of saints; few are capable of their degree of self-immolation, of their readiness to put on a back burner or downright ignore and neglect their own self-interest, or prepared for the volume of self-sacrifice which that responsibility would so often require as long as it stayed in its pristine, un-retouched state of 'unconditionality'. Besides, even if we were able and willing to take upon ourselves fully and truly unconditional and infinite responsibility, it would offer us poor guidance to resolving the innumerable conflicts of interests which human togetherness is bound to generate daily, and so to making shared life liveable. A viable society composed only of saints is for all practical purposes inconceivable, for the simple reason that one can't exercise full and unconditional responsibility for two people simultaneously in case, as may happen, their interests are at odds with each other. Whenever such a clash happens, there is no escape from weighing and comparing the relative entitlements of the quarrelling parties and giving the interests of one party some preference over those of another. In other words, responsibility has to stop short of true unconditionality.

This is, precisely, why in Levinas's opinion society is a must. Society, so Levinas insists, is a contraption to make a companionship of humans feasible, armed and burdened as they are with moral impulses and haunted by unconditional responsibility for each other. Society makes cohabitation feasible by trimming down the postulated unconditionality of responsibility and replacing *moral impulses* with *ethical norms* and procedural rules. Admittedly, even the most ingenious of social arrangements can't and wouldn't abolish the conflict between demands of living-in-society and the ethical demand. Despite any conceivable effort to the contrary, the modality of being a moral self will remain a harrowing, tormenting challenge devoid of truly satisfactory and/or ultimate, once-and-for-all, solutions and remedies. It is society, by codifying moral duties (and by the same token excluding large chunks of human interaction from moral obligations and censorship), and reducing thereby an infinite responsibility to the following of a finite set of rules, that makes life in common possible despite the conflict's unsolvability.

This effect (certainly a palliative, not a cure, let alone a definite one) is achieved through two closely related expedients. One consists, as already hinted, in replacing the infinite and unconditional, diffuse and incurably underdefined responsibility by a finite list of clearly spelled out duties – while relegating from the realm of moral obligations all that has been omitted from that list. In other words, society draws limits and spells out conditions where neither the first nor the second was postulated or indeed allowed by unconditional responsibility. This expedient is essentially a work of reduction; lopped of a great number of its densely packed and endlessly ramifying branches, 'responsibility for the Other', or more exactly whatever is left of it, is pulled back from the realm of excessive feats, 'beyond human capacity', to the size of humanly attainable, feasible and plausible duties. The ethical code so composed ostensibly serves the promotion of moral conscience and duty; but its genuine accomplishment is the exclusion from the universe of moral obligations certain kinds of 'others' and certain elements of 'otherness' for which moral persons will now be allowed to refuse to carry ethical responsibility, while being absolved or acquitted of moral guilt – and so also protected against the pangs of conscience which such a refusal might otherwise have caused.

But let me repeat, this expedient is a palliative, not a cure against the dilemmas and torments generated by the endemic unconditionality of moral responsibility: the kind of responsibility that is evoked in each of us and silently yet poignantly appealed to by the very sight of an Other in need of succour, care and love. The expedient of codifying ethical rules may protect the neglectful person from legal punishment, and even from public disapproval, but it will hardly deceive the conscience and excise the awareness, and so also the torments, of moral guilt. As the English proverb puts it, 'a guilty conscience needs no accuser'. Pointing to common standards as a valid excuse for one's own failings ('look around, everyone in my place would do the same!') will not placate a guilty conscience; as Levinas insists, my responsibility for you is always one step ahead of your responsibility for me. This is why the expedient in question needs to be supplemented by another: by an offer of substitutes for the self-sacrifice which the exercise of unconditional responsibility for the Other would time and again require. These are substitutes deputizing (and deemed to compensate) for the unoffered or withdrawn 'natural', yet costlier, manifestations of concern – like the offers of one's time, compassion, empathy, comprehension, care or love, all calling for a degree of self-sacrifice; tokens of assumed responsibility to be used in cases when responsibility was not, could not or would not in fact be assumed; tokens of *form* to be used in cases where the *substance* is in short supply.

It is in this second of the two expedients – in the design, production and supply of 'morality substitutes' – that the consumer market plays a crucial, if only a mediating role. It performs several functions indispensable for that expedient to be operative and effective: it offers material tokens of concern, sympathy, compassion, well-wishing, friendship and love. The consumer market adopts and assimilates the ever wider sphere of interhuman relations, including care for the Other, its organizing moral principle. In the process, it subjects the design and narrative of those relations to the categories invented to serve the regular recurrence of the encounters between marketed goods and their buyers, and so to secure the continuing circulation of commodities. It thereby prompts the defining traits of a moral attitude to be manifested, perceived, understood and accepted as another instance of that circulation, not qualitatively distinct from other instances, or more precisely taken or mistaken for their equivalents. That expedient renders the notoriously vague and irritatingly underdefined moral notion of 'self-sacrifice for the good of another' tangible and measurable, through applying of universally comprehensible and easily legible monetary criteria of magnitude, and attaching price tags to the acts of goodness. All in all, the expedient in question acts as a psycho-therapeutic institution fighting back against, and sometimes even preventing, the afflictions and ailments triggered by the frustration of moral impulse and perpetrated by guilty conscience and moral scruples.

We all know such salutary and therapeutic qualities of commodity markets only too well, and we know them from autopsy: from our own daily experience. We know the guilty feeling of being unable to spend enough time with our nearest and dearest, family and friends, to listen to their problems as attentively and compassionately as such problems require, to be 'always there for you', to be ready to abandon whatever we have been doing at that moment and rush to help or just share in sorrows and console. Such experiences become, if anything, ever more common in our hurried lives. Just one off-hand illustration of the trend: if twenty years ago 60 per cent of American families regularly had family dinners, only 20 per cent of American families now meet around dinner tables.

Most of us are overwhelmed with the worries arising from our daily relations with bosses, workmates or clients, and most of us take those worries with us, in our laptops and mobile phones, wherever we go – to our homes, for weekend strolls, in holiday hotels: we are never further than a phone call or a phone message from the office, constantly at people's beck and call. Connected perpetually to the office network as we are, we have no excuse for not using Saturday and Sunday to work on the report or the project ready to be delivered on Monday. 'Office closing time' never arrives. The once sacrosanct borderlines separating home from office, work time from so-called 'free time' or 'leisure time', have all but been effaced, and so each and every moment of life becomes a moment of choice – a grave choice, a painful and often seminal choice, a choice between career and moral obligations, work duties and the demands of all those people needing our time, compassion, care, help and succour.

Obviously, consumer markets won't resolve those dilemmas for us, let alone chase them away or render them null and void; and we don't expect them to give us any of those services. But they can, and are eager to help us to mitigate, even to quash the pangs of guilty conscience. They do it through the precious, exciting gifts on offer, which you can spy out in shops or on the internet, buy and use to make some of those people who are hungry for your love smile and rejoice – if only for a brief moment. We are trained to expect the gifts supplied by shops to compensate those people for all those face-to-face, hand-in-hand hours we should have offered them but didn't. The more expensive those gifts are, the greater the compensation the giver expects them to offer their recipients, and consequently the stronger is their placating and tranquillizing impact on the giver's own pangs of conscience.

Shopping thereby becomes a sort of moral act (and vice versa: moral acts lead by way of the shops). Emptying your wallet or debiting your credit card takes the place of the self-abandonment and self-sacrifice that moral responsibility for the Other requires. The side-effect, of course, is that by advertising and delivering commercialized moral painkillers, consumer markets only facilitate, instead of preventing, the fading, wilting and crumbling of interhuman bonds. Rather than helping to resist the forces which caused the bonds to fall into dust, they collaborate in the work of their emaciation and gradual destruction.

Just as physical pain signals an organic trouble and prompts urgent remedial actions, moral scruples signal the dangers threatening interhuman bonds – and would prompt a deeper reflection and more energetic and adequate action were they not tempered by market-supplied moral tranquillizers and painkillers. Our intentions to do good to others have been commercialized. And yet it is not the consumer markets that need to be charged with the main responsibility, let alone the sole responsibility for that having happened. By design or by default, consumer markets are *accessories* to the crime of causing interhuman bonds to fall apart: accessories both before and after that crime was committed . . .

The second interface between consumer markets and ethics is located inside the vast area of identity concerns and identification pursuits on which a good part of our life strategies and preoccupations nowadays tend to focus. Since one of the most salient features of life lived in a liquid modern setting is the endemic and seemingly incurable instability of social placement (no longer undetachably ascribed and no longer unequivocally (recognized, once-and-for-all) – as well as the unclarity of the criteria by which one's 'place in the world' can be authoritatively assessed, as well as of the agencies entitled to make the assessment binding – it is no wonder that the question of self-identity figures high on most individuals' life agenda. And just as in the case of that other issue generating acute uncertainty, the weakening and growing frailty of human bonds, the instability and insecurity of people's place in society attracts the acute attention of the consumer market – because this is an aspect of the human condition on which the suppliers of consumer goods can, and indeed do, most lavishly capitalize.

The trick is to reconcile what apparently would stay irreconcilable as long as only individually managed resources are deployed (that is, in the absence of means guaranteed, or promised to be guaranteed, by supra-individual forces being universally recognized and accepted): namely, to reconcile the (however short-lived) security of a selected identity with the certainty, or at least high likelihood, that it will be promptly replaced with another selection once the present one becomes insecure or loses its attraction. In short, to reconcile the ability to *hold on to* an identity with the ability to *change it* on demand – the ability to 'be oneself' with the capacity for 'becoming someone else'. It is the simultaneous possession of both capacities that the liquid modern setting requires, and it is the tools and tokens needed to exercise both capacities that the consumer markets promise to supply.

Again, the individual's needs and the offers of the market are – in this case, just as in the previously discussed encounter between consumerism and the discharge of moral responsibility – related as the chicken is to the egg: one is not conceivable without the other, though deciding which of the two is the cause and which is an effect is out of the question. And yet the case for the indispensability as much as for the desirability, trustworthiness and effectiveness of the services of the consumer market must be convincingly made. The ground has been already prepared for that case by establishing a link between moral care and consumer goods: what remains is to transplant the inclinations rooted and developed in the context of 'responsibility for the Other' into the context of 'responsibility for (and to) oneself'. 'You've earned it', 'you deserve it', 'you owe it to yourself', calls invoking the terms borrowed or stolen from the realm of moral obligations, need to be, and are, redeployed in legitimizing consumerist self-indulgence.

Whatever lingers of the ethical oddity of such an incongruous redeployment of the idea of moral responsibility and care tends to be covered up or excised by putting a moral gloss on self-indulgence: to do something, you first need to be somebody; and so to be capable of caring for others, you first need to acquire, protect and retain the resources such a capacity requires. And you can't meet that condition unless you take up the market's offer of the means to make yourself into a 'somebody'; that is, unless you are able and willing to go along with progress (read, the latest fashion) and unless you can be relied upon to remain flexible and adjustable, be determined to change yourself promptly whenever change is called for – stay solid in your attachment to fluidity; in short, unless you are well positioned and thus well armed to care for others effectively and render their well-being secure. As you already know how closely the latter is dependent on your access to consumer goods, it is obvious that in order to follow your moral inclinations you need to translate the postulate of 'being somebody' into the command to make sure that you can obtain all those goods, in the right quantity and of the right quality, that you'll need to face up to your responsibility for others. Margaret Thatcher, that unerring exegete of the market stalls philosophy, went on record rewriting the Gospel: stating that the Good Samaritan couldn't have been a good Samaritan if he had had no money . . .

In short, to be moral, you must buy goods; to buy goods, you need money; to acquire money, you need to sell yourself – at a good price and with a decent profit. You can't be a shopper unless you yourself become a commodity which people are willing to buy. And what you therefore need is an attractive, sellable identity. You owe it to yourself – because, QED, you owe it to others. Stop worrying about those loudmouths around who charge you with unprepossessingly selfish or downright iniquitous and hedonistic motives. If you are indeed selfish, you are selfish for altruistic reasons. What may to some simpletons look like self-indulgence is in fact an implementation of moral duty; or, at least, this is how you might respond, indignantly, when you were reprimanded for focusing your untapped moral energy on the care of your own body and image. Obviously, you can resort to such an argument, and to great effect, when you are scolded – noisily – by others; but you can do it even when you are censured – in whispers – by your own conscience.

In responding to such charges, one can gain added self-confidence from the market-induced belief that, after all, the commodities' sole *raison d'être* is the satisfaction they bring – and that the life task of a commodity has been fulfilled and its right to exist exhausted once that satisfaction stops, or a greater satisfaction can be drawn from its replacement with another commodity. That belief encourages a faster circulation of utilities, while advising against developing a lasting attachment and loyalty to any one of them.

With the boomeranging of moral care back to the carer, the difference between the recommended treatment of 'animate' and ordinary 'inanimate' commodities is all but effaced or denied moral significance. In both cases, the end of the satisfaction brought by a 'commodity', or a sharp fall, is tantamount to a termination of the residence permit inside the universe of moral obligations. Redirected to the self-improvement of the carer, moral impulses turn into one of the principal causes of the erosion and enfeeblement of interhuman bonds, as well as of our collective indifference to the accumulating evidence of ever more widespread and 'naturalized' practices of exclusion.

And the third interface between consumerism and ethics, a derivative or an 'unintended consequence' of the two discussed above, is the impact of consumerism on the sustainability of our shared home, planet earth. We now know all too well that the resources of the planet have limits and cannot be infinitely stretched. We know as well that the limited resources of the planet are too modest to accommodate the levels of consumption that are rising everywhere to meet the standards currently reached in the richest parts of the planet – the very standards by which the dreams and prospects, ambitions and postulates of the rest of the planet tend to be measured in the era of the information highway (according to some calculations, such a feat would require multiplying the resources of our planet by a factor of five; five planets instead of the single one we have would be needed). And yet the invasion and annexation of the realm of morality by consumer markets has burdened consumption with functions it can perform only by pushing levels of consumption ever higher. This is the principal reason for viewing 'zero growth' as measured by gross national product, the statistics of the quantity of money changing hands in buying and selling transactions, as little short of not only an economic, but also a social and political catastrophe. Largely because of those extra functions – linked to consumption neither by their nature nor through 'natural affinity' – the prospect of setting a limit to the rise in consumption, not to mention cutting it down to an ecologically sustainable level, seems both nebulous and abhorrent – something no 'responsible' political force (read, no party orientated to the nearest elections) would include in its policy agenda. It may be surmised that the commodification of ethical responsibilities, those major building materials and tools of human togetherness, combined with the gradual yet relentless decay of all alternative, non-market ways of manifesting it, is a much more formidable obstacle to the containment and moderation of consuming appetites than the non-negotiable prerequisites of biological and social survival.

Indeed, if the level of consumption determined by biological and social survival is by its nature stable, the levels required to gratify the other needs promised, expected and demanded to be serviced by consumption are, again by the nature of such needs, inherently upward-oriented and rising; the satisfaction of those added needs does not depend on maintaining stable standards, but on the speed and degree of their rise. Consumers turning to the commodity market in search of satisfying their moral impulses and fulfilling their self-identification (read, self-commodification) duties are obliged to seek value-and-volume differentials, and therefore this kind of 'consumer demand' is an overpowering and irresistible factor in the upward push. Just as the ethical responsibility for Others tolerates no limits, so the consumption vested with the task of venting and satisfying moral impulses resists any kind of constraint imposed on its extension. Having been harnessed to the consumerist economy, moral impulses and ethical responsibilities are recycled, ironically, into a most awesome hindrance when humanity finds itself confronted with arguably the most formidable threat to its survival: a threat which cannot be fought back against without a lot, perhaps an unprecedented amount, of voluntary self-constraint and readiness for self-sacrifice.

Once it is set and kept in motion by moral energy, the consumerist economy has only the sky as its limit. To be effective in the job it has assumed, it cannot allow itself to slow down its pace, let alone pause and stand still. It must consequently counterfactually assume, tacitly if not in so many words, the limitlessness of the planet's endurability and the infinity of its resources. From the beginning of the consumerist era, enlarging the loaf of bread was promoted as the patent remedy, indeed a foolproof prophylactic, against conflicts and squabbles around the loaf's redistribution. Effective or not in suspending hostilities, that strategy had to assume infinite supplies of flour and yeast. We are now nearing the moment when the falsity of that assumption and the dangers of clinging to it are likely to be exposed. This might be the moment for moral responsibility to be refocused on its primary vocation: that of mutual assurance of survival. In such a refocusing, the decommodification of the moral impulse seems, however, to be paramount among all the necessary conditions.

The moment of truth may be nearer than it may seem from the overflowing shelves of supermarkets, the websites strewn with commercial pop-ups and the choruses of self-improvement experts and counsellors advising us how to make friends and influence people. The point is how to precede and forestall its coming with a moment of self-awakening. Not an easy task, to be sure: it will take nothing less than for the universe of moral obligations to embrace the whole of humanity, complete with its dignity and well-being, as well as the survival of the planet, its shared home.

6

Privacy, secrecy, intimacy, human bonds – and other collateral casualties of liquid modernity

Alain Ehrenberg, a uniquely insightful analyst of the convoluted trajectory of the modern individual's short yet dramatic history, attempted to pinpoint the date of birth of the late modern cultural revolution (at least of its French branch) that ushered us into the liquid modern world which we continue to inhabit; to find a sort of equivalent for the Western cultural revolution to the salvo of the battleship *Aurora* when it gave the signal for the assault and capture of the Winter Palace and triggered seventy years of Bolshevik rule. Ehrenberg chose an autumnal Wednesday evening in the1980s, when a certain Vivienne, an 'ordinary French woman', declared during a TV talk show, and so in front of several million spectators, that since her husband Michel was afflicted by premature ejaculation, she had never experienced an orgasm in the whole of her married life.

What was revolutionary enough about Vivienne's pronouncement to justify Ehrenberg's choice? Two closely connected aspects. First, acts quintessentially, even eponymically, *private* were revealed and talked about *in public* – that is, in front of anyone who wished or just happened to listen. And second, a *public* arena, that is a space open to uncontrolled entry, was used to vent and thrash out a matter of thoroughly *private* significance, concern and emotion. Between them, these two genuinely revolutionary steps legitimized *public* use of a language developed for *private* conversations between a strictly limited number of selected persons:

of a language whose prime function had hitherto been to set the realm of the 'private' apart from that of the 'public'. More precisely, these two interconnected breakthroughs initiated the deployment in public, for the consumption and use of a public audience, of a vocabulary designed to be used for narrating private, subjectively lived through experiences (*Erlebnisse* as distinct from *Erfahrungen*). As the years went by, it became clear that the true significance of the event was an effacing of the once sacrosant division between the 'private' and the 'public' spheres of human bodily and spiritual life.

Looking back and with the benefit of hindsight, we can say that Vivienne's appearance in front of millions of French men and women, glued to their TV screens, also ushered the viewers, and through them all the rest of us, into a *confessional society*: a hitherto unheard-of and inconceivable kind of society in which microphones are fixed inside confessionals, those eponymical safeboxes and depositories of the most secret of secrets, the sort of secrets to be divulged only to God or his earthly messengers and plenipotentiaries; and in which loudspeakers connected to those microphones are perched on public squares, places previously meant for brandishing and thrashing out issues of shared interest, concern and urgency.

The advent of the confessional society signalled the ultimate triumph of privacy, that foremost modern invention – though also the beginning of its vertiginous fall from the peak of its glory. It was thus the hour of a victory that was Pyrrhic, to be sure: privacy invaded, conquered and colonized the public realm, but at the expense of losing its autonomy, its defining trait and its most cherished and hotly defended privilege.

But let us begin at the beginning, the better to comprehend the present-day twists of a plot as long as the modern era.

What is 'private'? Anything that belongs to the realm of 'privacy'. To find out what is understood by 'privacy' these days, let's consult Wikipedia, the website known to promptly and diligently seek and record whatever popular wisdom currently believes or accepts to be the truth of the matter; and to update its findings day in, day out, following closely on targets that are notorious for running faster than even the most dedicated of their pursuers. As we could read in the English-language version of Wikipedia on 14 July 2010, privacy

> is the ability of an individual or group to seclude themselves or information about themselves and thereby reveal themselves selectively . . . Privacy is sometimes related to anonymity, the wish to remain unnoticed or unidentified in the public realm. When something is private to a *person*, it usually means there is something within them that is considered inherently special or personally sensitive . . . Privacy can be seen as an aspect of security – one in which trade-offs between the interests of one group and another can become particularly clear.

And what, on other hand, is 'public arena'? A space with access open to anyone who wishes to enter, look and listen. Everything heard and seen in a 'public arena' can in principle be heard and seen by anybody. Considering that (to quote Wikipedia once more) 'the degree to which private information is exposed depends on how the public will receive this information, which differs between places and over time', keeping a thought, an event or an act private, and making any of them public, are obviously as much at cross-purposes as they are interdependent (because of determining the limits of each other): the lands of the 'private' and the 'public' tend to be on a war footing, as do the laws and norms of decency prevailing inside those realms. For each of the two realms, the act of self-definition and self-assertion is performed in opposition to the other.

As a rule, the semantic fields of the two notions are not separated from each other by borders inviting or allowing two-way traffic, but by frontlines – preferably tightly sealed and heavily fortified on both sides against trespassers and turncoats as well as lukewarms preferring to sit on the barricade – but most particularly against deserters from either camp. Yet even if war hasn't been declared and warlike actions have not been undertaken (or if hostilities have been suspended), the boundary that separates private and public affairs only as a rule tolerates *selective* cross-traffic: free-for-all traffic would defy the very notion of a boundary and render the boundary redundant. Control, and the right to decide who or what is allowed to pass over the border and who or what must be stuck on only one side, and so also the right to decide what items of information are to have the prerogative of remaining private and which ones are allowed, pushed or decreed to become public, are as a rule hotly contested. If you wish to know which side is presently on the offensive and which is (pugnaciously or half-heartedly) trying to defend its inherited or acquired rights against invaders, you could do worse than ponder on the prophetic foreboding (expressed in 1956) of Peter Ustinov: 'This is a free country, madam. *We* have a right to share *your* privacy in a public space' (emphasis added).

For most of the modern era the assault on the current private–public frontier, and still more importantly univocal revocations and arbitrary changes in the prevailing rules governing border traffic, were almost exclusively expected or feared to come from the 'public' side: public institutions were widely suspected of an intention to invade and conquer the sphere of the private and take it under their administration, and thereby to severely curtail the realm of free will and free choice, depriving human individuals or groups of individuals of shelter and, as a consequence, of personal or group security. The most sinister and harrowing demons haunting the times of 'solid modernity' were succinctly yet vividly portrayed in George Orwell's trope of the 'jackboot trampling down the human face'.

Somewhat inconsistently but yet not groundlessly, public institutions were suspected of evil intentions or malicious practices in erecting barricades blocking many a private concern its access to the agora or to other sites of the free exchange of information – sites where a raising of private troubles to the level of public issues could be negotiated. Obviously, the gruesome record of the two similarly rapacious and cruel twentieth-century varieties of totalitarianism (which, as if to top despair with hopelessness, seemed to have exhausted between them the spectrum of imaginable choices: one variety claiming the legacy of the Enlightenment and its modern project, and the other decrying that foundational act of modernity as a sorry mistake or a crime, and rejecting the modern project as a recipe for disaster) lent veracity to those suspicions and so also justification to the resulting anxiety.

Though by now past their peak, such suspicions linger, and anxiety refuses to abate – galvanized time and again, resuscitated and reinvigorated by news of one or another public institution arbitrarily transferring another larger swathe of its own *functions* and obligations from the 'public' to the 'private' realm, in blatant violation of usages firmly entrenched in the democratic mentality even if they were uncodified, while openly or surreptitiously transferring in the opposite direction, collecting, and storing for future villainous uses ever bigger volumes of indisputedly private *information*. And yet, whatever the case of the assumed greed and rapacity of the public realm, and of its imputed or anticipated aggressiveness, and however the perceptions of each might have been changing over time, alarms about an impending invasion and conquest of the public sphere by private interests and concerns were at best few and far between. The task inspiring most of our ancestors and older generations to take arms was one of defending the private domain, and so individual autonomy, from undue meddling by the powers that be.

Until recently, that is: because today, triumphant reports of the 'liberation' of successive areas of public territory by the advancing troops of the private, greeted with applause and jubilation by avidly and joyfully watching crowds, are mixed with sombre premonitions (thus far faint) and with warnings (thus far sparse and tentative) that the ostensible 'liberation' bears all the marks of an imperialist conquest, a ruthless occupation and greedy colonialism . . .

On *secrecy* (and so obliquely on privacy, individuality, autonomy, self-definition and self-assertion – secrecy being an indispensable, crucial and undetachable ingredient of them all), Georg Simmel, that most penetrating and far-sighted scholar among the founders of sociology, observed that to stand a realistic chance of surviving intact it needs to be *acknowledged by others*.[1] A rule needs to be observed that 'what is intentionally or unintentionally hidden is intentionally or unintentionally respected'. The relationship between these two conditions (of privacy and the capacity for self-determination and self-assertion) tends to be unstable and tense, however – and 'the intention of hiding' 'takes on a much greater intensity when it clashes with the intention of revealing'. What follows from Simmel's observation is that if this 'greater intensity' fails to emerge, if the urge to defend what is secret tooth and nail against interlopers, meddlers and busybodies disrespectful of one's secrets is absent, *privacy is in danger*. And this is exactly what now happens, as Peter Ustinov, updating Georg Simmel's pronouncement, picked up from the mood of our times – times only younger by a few decades than those of Simmel's study.

Occasional warnings of the terminal dangers to privacy and individual autonomy that emanate from the opening wide of the public arena to private concerns, and its gradual yet relentless transformation into a sort of light entertainment variety theatre, produce few if any repercussions on the public agenda and, in particular, in popular attention. The paradox of 'deregulation' (read, the voluntary relinquishing by the state of a great number of the competences it jealously guarded in the past), coupled with 'individualization' (read, the abandonment of a great number of the state's past duties to the individually managed and operated realm of 'life politics'), both advertised as the royal road to the ultimate victory of individual rights – but in fact sapping the foundations of individual autonomy while stripping that autonomy of the past attractions which used to raise it to the rank of a most coveted value – is all but covered up in the process, attracting little if any attention and triggering little if any action.

Secret, by definition, is that part of knowledge whose sharing with others is refused or prohibited and/or closely controlled. Secrecy, as it were, draws and marks the boundary of privacy, privacy being the realm that is meant to be one's own domain, the territory of one's undivided sovereignty, inside which one has the comprehensive and indivisible power to decide 'what and who I am' – and from which one may launch and relaunch campaigns to have and keep one's decisions recognized and respected. In a startling U-turn from the habits of our ancestors, we have lost the guts, the stamina and above all the will to persist in the defence of such rights, those irreplaceable building blocks of individual autonomy. In our day, it is not so much the possibility of a betrayal or violation of privacy that frightens us, but the opposite: a shutting down of the exits. The area of privacy is turning into a site of incarceration, the owner of private space being condemned and doomed to stew in his or her own juice; forced into a condition marked by the absence of avid listeners eager to wring out our secrets and tear them from behind the ramparts of privacy, to put them on public display, to make them everybody's shared property and a property everybody wishes to share. *We seem to experience no joy in having secrets*, unless they are the kind of secrets likely to enhance our egos by attracting the attention of the researchers and editors of TV talk-shows, tabloid front pages and the covers of glossy magazines.

As a result of all that, it is now the public sphere that finds itself flooded, overcrowded and overwhelmed, having become a target of continuous invasion, occupation and colonization by the troops of privacy. But are those troops leaving their past shelters – barracks, stockades and fortresses – prompted by the urge to conquer new outposts and spawn new garrisons, or are they rather running away, in despair and panic, from their customary safe enclosures, now found to be no longer habitable? Is their zeal a symptom of a newly acquired spirit of exploration and conquest, or rather an outcome of, and a testimony to, expropriation and victimization? Is the task they have been ordered to perform in our liquid modern times – the task of finding out and/or deciding 'what and who I am' – too daunting to be seriously undertaken inside the meagre allotments of privacy? After all, the evidence is piling up by the day that the harder one tries to experiment with successive tentative attempts and to laboriously patch up successive public images, the less likely is the prospect of reaching the self-assurance and self-confidence whose promise triggered all these exertions . . .

This is only one of the questions with no obvious answer. There is another question, though, also still waiting in vain for an answer. Secrecy, after all, is not only a tool of privacy, used to cut out a space entirely of one's own, to set oneself apart from intruders and unwelcome companions; it is also a most powerful tool for building and servicing togetherness, for tying together and protecting arguably the strongest of the known and conceivable interhuman bonds. By confiding one's secrets to some selected, 'very special' people while barring them from all the others, webs of friendship are woven, one's 'best friends' are appointed and retained, infinite commitments are entered into and maintained (indeed, blank cheques are signed, in so far as the commitments are indeterminate and lack a withdrawal clause); loose aggregates of individuals are recast into tightly knit and firmly integrated, possibly long-lasting, groups. In short, enclaves are cut out of the world inside which the troublesome and vexing clash between belonging and autonomy is for once laid to rest; in which the choices between private interest and the well-being of others, between altruism and selfishness, self-love and care for others, stop their torment and no longer foment and fan the painful and infuriatingly repetitive pangs of conscience.

But, as Thomas Szasz already observed in *The Second Sin* in 1973, while focusing on just one, but an immensely effective, tool of human bonding, 'traditionally, sex has been a very private, secretive activity. Herein perhaps lies its powerful force for uniting people in a strong bond. As we make sex less secretive, we may rob it of its power to hold men and women together.' Sexual pursuits served until recently as a genuine epitome of intimate secrets, meant to be shared with the utmost discretion and with only the most carefully and laboriously selected others. In other words, they offered a prime example of the strongest of interhuman bonds, the ones most difficult to cut and take apart, and therefore the most reliable. But what applies to that most effective weapon and guardian of privacy applies even more to its lesser companions, inferior substitutes and paler copies. *The present day crisis of privacy is inextricably connected with the weakening and decay of all and any interhuman bonds.*

In this intertwining between the collapse of privacy and the falling apart of bonds, one factor is the egg and the other the chicken, and it is waste of time to quarrel about which is the first and which came second . . .

Quite a few observers, and the popular wisdom following their suggestions, have recently invested the hope of fulfilling the twin promises of meeting the demands of individual self-assertion and community building, while simultaneously defusing the conflict between autonomy and belonging, in cutting edge technology, with its astonishing capacity to facilitate interhuman contact and communication. Frustration of that hope is gathering force, however, and spreading.

That frustration is perhaps an unavoidable price of the accelerated passage of information offered by the creation of the 'information highway', as the internet has been called. All kinds of newly laid highways tempt more people to obtain vehicles, to use them, and to use them more often; hence the highways rapidly tend to become overcrowded (they, so to speak, invite, create, and beef up overcrowding), which defies their original promise. Getting travellers to the planned destinations more quickly and with less effort may prove to be a much more harrowing task than was expected. In the case of the 'information highways', however, there is another powerful reason for frustration: the destination of messages, the 'vehicles' rushing and dashing along this kind of highway, is after all *human attention*, which the internet is unable to expand, just as it cannot stretch its capacity to consume and digest. On the contrary, adjusting to the conditions created by the internet makes attention frail and above all shifting, unable to stay still for long, drilled and accustomed to 'surf' but not to fathom, to 'zap' through channels but not to wait until any of the plots zapped over is revealed in its full width and depth. In short, attention tends to be trained to skate over the surface much faster than would be needed to get a glimpse of what hides beneath.

To stand a chance of being noted at all, electronic messages must therefore be shortened and simplified, in order to deliver all their content before attention wilts or breaks away and drifts elsewhere; this is a necessity that makes them utterly unsuitable for conveying profound ideas needing reflection and contemplation. That tendency to shorten and simplify messages, to make them ever more shallow and therefore still more amenable to being surfed over, has marked the brief yet stormy history of the worldwide web from the start. From long, elaborate and thoughtful letters to emails, from brief yet juicy emails to yet more curtailed and simplified iPhone 'texting', and onto 'twittering' allowing no more than 140 digits . . . If you apply to the electronic world the Darwinian principle of the 'survival of the fittest' (or Copernicus' perception and Gresham's law stating that 'bad money drives out good'), the information most likely to reach human attention is the briefest, the shallowest and the least burdened with meaning; sentences rather than elaborate arguments, single buzz-words rather than sentences, 'sound-bites' rather than words. The price we all pay for more information being 'available' is a shrinking of its meaning content; the price of its ready availability is a radical reduction in its significance.

The other, though closely related ambivalence endemic to the new information technology comes from the immense facilitation of community *formation* arriving in a package deal with the equally immense facilitation of its *dismantling*. Users of Facebook's services boast of making five hundred 'new friends' in a day – more than I've managed in a life eighty-five years long . . . But does this mean that when we speak of 'friends' we have in mind the same kind of relationship?

Unlike the formation for which the name 'community' (or for that matter any other concept referring to the public side of human existence, the 'totality' of human association) was first coined, internet 'communities' *are not meant for durability*, let alone being commensurate with the duration of time. They are easy to join; but they are similarly easy to leave and abandon the moment that attention, sympathies and antipathies, and moods or fashions, drift in a different direction; or the moment that the boredom of 'more of the same, always the same' sets in, making the current state of affairs look dreary and feel unappetizing, as sooner or later it will in a lifeworld bombarded by ever new (and ever more tempting and seductive) offers. Internet communities (recently, and more accurately, called 'networks') are composed and decomposed, enlarged or cut down in size, by the multiple acts of individual decisions and impulses to 'connect' and 'disconnect'. They are therefore eminently changeable, fragile and incurably fissiparous – and this is precisely why so many people, cast in the liquid modern setting, welcome their arrival and prefer them to the 'old style' communities, remembered as monitoring their members' daily conduct, keeping them on a short leash, fighting every sign of their disloyalty and even minute misdemeanours, and making a change of mind and a decision to leave either impossible or exorbitantly costly. It is precisely their perpetual state of transience, their admittedly temporary because eternally provisional nature, their abstention from requiring long-term (let alone unconditional) commitments or undivided loyalty and strict discipline, that make them so attractive to so many – given the fluid surroundings for which the liquid modern form of life is so noted.

The substitution of internet networks for old-style communities was greeted by many as a huge leap forward in the history of individual liberty of choice. And yet the same features of networks that make them desirable require a high price which many people, in growing numbers, find unpalatable and unendurable; a price paid in the currency of security, which old-style communities delivered but internet 'networks' are incapable of credibly promising. Moreover, this is not just a case of exchanging one value for another, 'a bit of security for a bit of freedom'. The demise of the old-style communities contributes to the liberation of the individual, but the liberated individuals may well find it impossible, or at least beyond their individual capacity and the capacity of the resources they individually command, to make sensible use of their decreed freedom – to be not just free de jure, but also de facto. The allegedly fair exchange is seen by its many presumed beneficiaries as rendering them much more helpless and hapless, and for that reason *more insecure* . . .

To sum up, it may be surmised that the task of making individual liberty genuine calls for a strengthening, rather than a weakening, of the bonds of interhuman solidarity. The long-term commitment which strong solidarity promotes may seem a mixed blessing – but so does an absence of commitments that renders solidarity as unreliable as it makes it uninhibiting . . .

The cohabitation of the private and the public is full of sound and fury. And yet without their co-presence human togetherness is no more conceivable than water without the co-presence of hydrogen and oxygen. Each of the co-present partners needs the other to stay in a viable and wholesome condition; in their kind of cohabitation a war of attrition is tantamount to the suicide of both. Now, as in the past and in the future, self-care and care for the well-being of the other point in the same direction and recommend the same life philosophy and strategy. This is why the search for a settlement between private and public is unlikely ever to grind to halt. Neither are the sound and the fury that mark their relations.

7

Luck and the individualization
of remedies

According to the *Oxford English Dictionary*, 'luck' might originally have been a gambling term: that is, invented and introduced to describe something that might happen to someone addicted to hazard, to a gambling person, but which could have been different from what it was, or might not have happened at all; in other words, something neither certain to occur nor predictable – and, most importantly, unconnected to anything the gambler could or had to do, except joining the game and so 'taking a chance', as the rest of players did.

Indeed, 'luck' was a happening that couldn't be ascribed to a specific 'cause': to an act or event that 'determined' it, made that happening inevitable, unavoidable, a necessity – unless cancelled or modified by interference from some meddlesome, yet invisible and impervious power, like Fortuna, the goddess of chance, or a secret office or scheming gang with the capacity to decide in some mysterious way the ups and downs of the human lot, in the manner of an omnipotent, superhuman and divine force, as in the popular proverb, 'man proposes but God disposes'. A win was a case of *good* luck, a loss (and particularly an unusually long run of losses) a case of *bad* luck; but both occurred for no obvious reason and none was anticipated with any self-assurance, let alone certainty.

Good or ill, luck is the very *opposite of certainty*. Speaking of 'luck' presumes an essentially uncertain setting: an underdetermined or underdefined setting, neither preordained nor pre-empted (not a 'foregone conclusion'), but above all immune and insensitive to one's own intentions and undertakings. A setting, in other words, in which anything may happen yet the consequence of no undertaking can be reliably predicted. 'Uncertainty' defies our capacity to comprehend the situation, act with self-confidence and pursue and reach the purposes we set.

In other words, the state of uncertainty, that home ground of gambling and of good or bad luck, is a joint product of *ignorance* and *impotence* – the two dragons which the Enlightenment heirs of St George promised, resolved and tried hard to kill, or at least to chase away from the world of human beings and bar their return. 'Ignorance' in this case means disconnection between what we expect, hope and desire to happen, and what actually happens. 'Impotence' means the disconnection between what we are able to accomplish, and what we should or would wish to achieve.

We *feel uncertain* when we do not fully know the sorts of factors that make our situation what it is, and so we do not know the factors that need to be deployed and set in motion to make that situation more agreeable – or the factors needed to prevent it from getting worse; we *feel impotent* once we have learned or come to suspect that even if we had drawn up a full inventory of such factors, we would nonetheless have lacked the tools, the skills, or the resources to set them in motion, or to disable them if need be. Instead of strengthening our hand and emboldening us, the knowledge we acquire will therefore humiliate us, by exposing how inadequate we are to the task. This is why feeling simultaneously uncertain and impotent is such a thoroughly unpleasant, irritating and disgraceful, insulting and humiliating condition to be in. This is also why we've come to see the twin promises – of science to replace ignorance with knowledge, and of technology to replace impotence with the power to act effectively – as two of the most magnificent, if not *the* most magnificent, glories of the modern era.

Modernity arrived as the promise and determination to conquer uncertainty; or at least to wage a total war of attrition against that many-headed monster. Philosophers of the Enlightenment explained the sudden abundance of uncomfortable and frightening surprises, mishaps and miseries inflicted by the uncontrolled forces let loose by protracted religious wars, stubbornly escaping the weakening grip of local checks and balances, by the retreat of God from daily management of his creation – or by a flaw in Creation itself: namely, the vagaries and caprices to which Nature was prone in its raw state, so evidently alien and deaf to human needs and wishes, as long as it was untamed and unbridled by human ingenuity, reason and labour. The preferred explanations might have differed, yet broad agreement gradually emerged that the prevailing administration of wordly affairs had failed its test, and that the world urgently needed to be taken under new, this time *human*, management. This new management was instructed and resolved, to put paid to the most awesome demons of uncertainty once and for all: to contingency, randomness, lack of clarity, ambivalence, underdetermination and unpredictability. The declared aim of the managerial change was to subordinate obstreperous and wanton Nature (including *human* nature) to the rule of reason; more to the point, to remake Nature (again including human nature) after the pattern of Reason – which, as everyone should know, is animated and guided by its inborn and unconditional enmity to contradiction, ambiguity and all sorts of abnormality, as well as by its unswerving loyalty to the precepts of order, norm and obedience to law; in short, a rule of reason able to design in due time the means needed to impose on the natural and human worlds a pattern made to the measure of human needs and preferences. Once that job was brought to completion, the human world would no longer be dependent on strokes of luck. Instead of being a welcome yet inexplicable and unsolicited gift of fate, human happiness would be a regular product of planning based on knowledge and its applications. Once modernity had delivered on its promise, you would no longer have to rely on luck for your well-being and happiness.

Human management failed to rise to popular expectations, however beefed up they were by the lavish assurances of its learned advocates and court poets. True, many inherited arrangements accused of contaminating human pursuits with uncertainty were dismantled and disposed of, but the patterns put in their place turned out to produce just as much uncertainty – while in a growing number of situations the outcomes from the recommended rules of conduct proved to depend on chance. The number of unknown variables in the equations of human life showed no sign of diminishing. The hoped for and promised certainty, deemed so predictable, was nowhere in sight, staying stubbornly beyond the reach of its pursuers.

For the first one or two hundred years of the war against uncertainty, the absence of a convincing victory could be overlooked, or at least played down. Suspicions that uncertainty could be a permanent, indelible and inseparable companion of human existence tended to be dismissed as wrong in principle, or at least grossly premature. Despite growing evidence to the contrary, it was still possible to prognosticate that certainty would indeed appear over the horizon once the next, or the next but one, corner was turned. The objective might have proved more remote than it had seemed in the heady juvenile years of the modern era, but the delay, however disappointing, neither devalued the objective nor testified to its unattainability; at the utmost, it presented the task as more difficult to achieve than previously supposed, and therefore calling for still more ingenuity, effort, funds and sacrifice. The continuing presence of contingency could still be explained away by an insufficiency of knowledge attained thus far, or by regrettable yet rectifiable errors of management – rather than calling for a substantive rethinking of the assumed and postulated destination of the modern adventure.

During the last half century, however, a drastic change gathered impetus in our world view: this change reached far beyond our conception of the role of contingency in human history and the life itinerary of individuals, and our belief in the imminent mitigation of its impact brought by the progress of knowledge and technology. In the most recent narratives of the origins and development of the universe as a whole, or of the origins and evolution of life on earth, as much as in our descriptions of the elementary units of matter, random irregular events – essentially unpredictable because underdetermined or altogether contingent – have been upgraded from the rank of freak and marginal 'disturbances' or 'abnormalities' to that of constantly present factors and principal explanations.

The modern idea of social engineering rested its trustworthiness on the presupposition of indomitable 'depth rules', thus far undiscovered and poorly understood, yet bound to be brought to surface by the work of reason; of iron laws governing nature and making human existence orderly and fully regular once the contingencies causing turbulence were swept out of their way. But in the last half century or so it has been the very existence of 'iron laws', and the very plausibility (indeed conceivability) of unbroken chains of cause and effect, that have come to be questioned – and increasingly doubted. We are coming to realize that contingency, randomness, haphazardness, ambiguity and irregularity are not products of occasional and in principle rectifiable blunders, but inalienable features of all existence; and so also unremovable from the social and individual lives of humans. Natural sciences and human sciences seem for once to converge on remarkably similar opinions about the existential modality of their respective objects. It is as if the train of scientific thought in its totality has been, by design or default, redirected under the impact of drastic changes in the human living experience and life practices and ambitions . . .

The direction in which the train of scholarly thought seems to be going since taking that turn is bringing it close to the conclusions reached quite a while ago by Jorge Luis Borges in his philosophical reflection on the randomness of rewards and punishments, falling on people without any connection whatsoever to what they are doing or what they have neglected to do. It looked, said Borges, in his story called 'Lottery in Babylon', that somewhere in the City cellars a clandestine Corporation was hiding, distributing good and bad turns of fate simply by drawing lots, as all lotteries do. Borges listed a number of theories developed by the beneficiaries and victims of successive draws in order to find some order in what was by all standards disorderly turns of events – only to conclude in the end that 'it makes no difference whether one affirms or denies the reality of the shadowy corporation, because Babylon is nothing but an infinite game of chance'. . .

What Borges suggests – and we have no good reasons to deny it and no hard arguments to refute it – is that we are doomed to bathe forever in that unsavoury concoction of ignorance and impotence from which our reflections started – whichever Babylon we happen to inhabit. However much we try to subordinate the effects of our actions to our intentions and conduct, time and again they differ widely from our expectations, and we find ourselves incapable of deciding beforehand when and how different this or that effect of our moves will be. It is precisely *as if* there was a secret corporation bent on keeping effects separate from causes, and outcomes of actions separate from their intentions. Or perhaps there is no link between the causes and effects, intentions and outcomes of our actions; perhaps such a link exists only in our imagination, hungry as we are for order and logic, and so there is nothing to be found, no 'knowledge' to liberate us from our ignorance; no 'depth rules' and regularities we can discover and memorize in order never again to err and be frustrated, and in order to make sure that good things come our way *whenever* we stretch out our hands to reach them? As Borges would respond, 'it makes no difference'. From wherever it comes and whoever may run it, the 'infinite game of chance' allows no escape. A state of certainty is a figment of fanciful imagination aided, abetted and beefed up by the horrors of ubiquitous and continuous uncertainty: a dream dreamt by uncertain and insecure people who may be aware that it is a dream but be unable to stop dreaming it. The less certain and therefore less secure we feel, the more intense our dreams and the more desperate our search for substitutes, palliatives, half-measures, tranquillizers – anything to dampen fear of the unknown and postpone looking one's own impotence in the face. 'Luck' figures high on the list of such expedients.

And in our liquid modern times there are plenty of reasons, many more than only fifty years ago, to feel uncertain and insecure. I say 'feel', because we cannot be sure if the volume of uncertainties has grown: what we can ascertain is that the volume of our concerns and worries has. And it has because the gaps between our means of effective action and the grandiosity of the tasks we confront and are obliged to handle has become more evident, more obvious and indeed more blatant and frightening these days than it looked to our fathers and grandfathers. It is our newly perceived impotence that makes our uncertainty feel more ghastly and menacing than before.

Two of the aforementioned gaps seem particularly abysmal and unbridgeable. One comes into our vision whenever we raise our heads upwards, hoping to spy out some potent forces 'up there' which we can call on (in hope!) to come to our rescue and protect us against blows of misfortune. We scan earth and heaven with little success, hardly ever finding what are we looking for, while our calls for help remain by and large unanswered. As to the other gap we are forced to deal with daily, it stretches between where we *are* and where we wish, feel we should, are tempted or are commanded *to be*; but in most cases we find the gap between the two banks of the dividing ravine much too wide to leap over.

The first gap arose as a result of the divorce between power and politics. 'Power' is a shorthand expression for the ability to do things – whereas 'politics' signifies the ability to decide what things ought to be done (that is, for what purposes available power should be used). Until quite recently power and politics resided and closely cooperated inside the offices of the nation-state: that made politics conducted by the sovereigns of the nation-state powerful, while casting power under control of politics. Their separation and pending divorce came as a surprise: both the forces eager to reform and the forces bent on preserving the status quo, after all, counted on the state organs to be reliable and adequate executors of their intentions and the right vehicles for their intended actions. 'Progressive' and 'conservative' forces quarrelled about *what* was to be done, whereas the question of *who is to do it* hardly ever worried them. To both forces, institutions deciding political programmes were the most powerful and adequate organs of actions and bound to remain so – as the sovereignty of the state on its territory was acknowledged as absolute, indivisible and uncontestable.

The above is no longer the case, though. Many, perhaps most of the powers operated by the state political institutions 'evaporated' into the (as Manuel Castells put it) 'space of flows' – the no-man's land stretching beyond the reach of any state or combination of states. They are powerful enough and mobile enough to play down or ignore state borders, local interests and territorially binding laws and rules of action. Powers drawing the borderline between realistic and non-realistic options have been emancipated from most of the constraints which the territorial powers of nation-states are able to impose or indeed to contemplate. At that global level, the discrepancy between available means and postulated objectives of action takes the form of a perpetual confrontation between politics afflicted by a chronic deficit of power, and power freed from politically imposed limitations.

The second gap arose at the other extreme of the power hierarchy: at the level of (to use Anthony Giddens's terms) 'life politics'. As powers to act effectively slipped from their fingers, the weakened states were obliged to surrender to the pressures of global powers and 'subsidiarize' a growing number of functions they previously performed to individuals' wit, care and responsibility. As Ulrich Beck pointed out, it is now individuals, each one on her or his own, who are expected to seek and find individual answers to socially created problems, act upon them using their individually managed resources, and bear responsibility for their choices and the success or defeat of their actions; in other words, we are now all 'individuals by decree', commanded and assumed to be capable of designing our lives and mustering everything needed to pursue and see through our life objectives.

For most of us, our assumed power to get things done seems suspect – fully, or at least in large part, a fiction. Most of us lack the resources needed to raise ourselves from the status of 'individuals by decree' to the rank of 'individuals de facto'. We lack both the needed *knowledge* and the required *potency*. Our ignorance and impotence in finding individual solutions to socially produced problems result in a loss of self-esteem, the shame of inadequacy and the pains of humiliation. All that combines in the experience of a continuous and incurable state of haplessness fed by uncertainty: an inability to take one's life under one's own control, being thereby condemned to a condition not unlike that of the plankton buffeted by tides of unknown origin, timing, direction and intensity.

Living under a cloud of ignorance and impotence, in surroundings dripping with uncertainties, enormously benefits the current comeback of the category of 'luck', restoring it to a public favour once withdrawn and denied on account of luck's close kinship with contingency, accident, randomness and other abominations which modernity swore to make redundant and sweep out of human lives. From a handicap, luck's affinity with the factors of disorder and blind chance has turned into an asset. Indeed, once the ostensibly omniscient and omnipotent institutions – having promised to streamline the convoluted trajectory of human destiny into a string of orderly and controllable, teachable and learnable, patterned and predictable moves – had failed to deliver on their promise, demand grew for alternative ideas capable of rendering existence, in part if not fully, comprehensible, manageable – and liveable. Luck, chance, opportunity were the obvious candidates for the role of such substitute ideas. The resounding resonance between the images they invoked and first-hand experience of daily life spoke – and goes on speaking – in their favour. After all, we all seem to live today in Borges' Babylon, as it were, ruled by the drawing of lots in an unknown, invisible lottery run by an unknown, invisible Corporation. Or, as George Steiner baptized the code by which we live, we live in a casino culture . . .

With the ideal of certainty located beyond our individual and collective reach, and increasingly recognized to be so, probability seemed to be the second-best choice in the search for substitute ideas. We can't say what will happen in any one particular case of doing this or that, but what we can be 'pretty certain' of is that if we repeat doing this or that many times in a row, a calculable quantity of attempts will bring us success (for instance, the greater the number of attempts to cast a die, the better are the chances of every one of its six faces of coming on top; no wonder that a popular English way to describe an absolutely honest, crystal-clear person is 'as straight as a die'). We cannot predict the outcome of any one of our moves, but we can calculate the probability of the outcomes being successful; and conversely, we can calculate the probability of them failing – in other words, the 'risk of failure'. The tacit assumption underlying such a hope is that in a sufficiently large number of trials the effects of disturbing factors like accidents will so to speak 'cancel each other out'. And once our calculations are done, we can select the kind of move that makes success more probable than other moves do. Had not Seneca this in mind when he famously suggested that 'luck comes to the prepared'?

If the category of certainty has no room for strokes of luck or blows of bad fortune, the idea of risk can't do without them – as every roulette player can testify, having learned the hard way that though the probabilities of red and black numbers coming out are exactly even, that does not stop you from losing an awful lot of money if you stubbornly bet on the red during a series of fifteen or more black numbers in a row. If it follows from the calculation of probabilities that in every thousand roulette games you can expect five hundred wins for red numbers, you still need luck if you want a red number to come out when you put your bet on it. Remember, the exactitude (and so the reliability) of risk calculations grows with the volume of repeated attempts; but it is highly unlikely that you will be able to afford to repeat them a thousand times, let alone go on repeating them infinitely – and even if you could do that, you still wouldn't know whether the money you won covered the costs of the 'unlucky' trials . . .

This is not the sole snag, however, that makes trust in a risk calculation a very poor alternative to belief in iron-clad laws of nature that predetermine and preempt results, or in an 'ordered' human society. It is not, after all, endlessly repeating occurrences that inspire us to resort to notions of good or bad luck in order to grasp at least some feasibility of logic in surprising turns of events. What frightens us most is the likelihood of being taken by surprise, unawares, by a one-off catastrophe, and so a type of occurrence that escapes any calculation of risk based on high numbers of repetitive happenings, and that in addition would defy our powers of defence even if it were guessed in advance. A sudden transfer to a distant land of a production line that used to provide you and your neighbours with your means of livelihood will not be made more avoidable by the most pedantic calculations of probabilities: no more avoidable than the next tsunami, volcano eruption, earthquake, or poisonous oil spill. Calculations of risk may help in a world marked by regularity. But irregularity is the trademark of the world we inhabit.

So at the far end of the long string of battles waged by modernity against the rule of 'mere chance', we chance to witness the triumphant comeback of 'luck' well before it arrived at the place of exile where it had been sentenced to remain from here to eternity . . .

8

Seeking in modern Athens an answer to the ancient Jerusalem question

Carl Schmitt's *Political Theology* (conceived in 1922 and recycled ten years later, with the rest of the t's crossed and the rest of the i's dotted, into *The Concept of the Political*) was meant to be to political theory what the Book of Job has been to Judaism, and through Judaism to Christianity.

It was intended, designed and hoped to answer one of the most notoriously haunting of the questions 'born in Jerusalem': the kind of question with which the most famous of the ideas born in Jerusalem – the idea of a monocentric world, ruled by a *one and only God*, the omnipresent and omnipotent creator of stars, mountains and seas, judge and saviour of the whole earth and the whole of humanity – could not but be pregnant. That question would hardly occur elsewhere – in particular to Athenians living in a world crowded with larger and smaller deities of larger or smaller nations; though it would not occur to ancient, 'tribal god' Hebrews either, at least as long as their god, much like the god of the Greeks, shared the earth (even their own tiny homeland, Canaan) with uncountable gods of hostile tribes. That question would not be asked by Hebrews, however, even if their god claimed planet-wide mastery, since the Book of Job predesigned the answer before the question could be fully articulated and start to haunt them in earnest. That answer, let us recall, could not be simpler: *The Lord gave, the Lord took away, blessed be His name.* Such an answer called for resigned obedience, but no questioning or debate; it needed neither learned commentary nor profuse foot-notes to sound convincing. The question with which the idea of a one-and-only God was pregnant, however, had to be born once the Hebrew Prophet Jesus declared the omnipotent God to be in addition the God of Love, and when his disciple St Paul brought the Good Tidings to Athens – a place where questions, once asked, were expected to be answered, and in tune with the rules of logic. That the answer was not available off-hand shows the rather unwelcoming reception which St Paul received among the Athenians, and the fact that when addressing 'the Greeks' he pre-ferred to send his missives to the much less philosophically sophis-ticated Corinthians . . .

In the world of the Greeks (a polycentric world like the worlds of the countless other polytheistic peoples) there was a separate god for every human pursuit and experience, and for every situa-tion and life occasion, and so there was also an answer to each past and future query – and above all an explanation for every and any past and current inconsistency in divine actions, and a recipe for improvising new, yet a priori sensible, explanations in case new inconsistencies were spotted. To pre-empt or at least retrospectively neutralize divine defiance of human logic, many gods were needed: gods aiming at cross-purposes, just as humans do; gods quarrelling with each other, making havoc of other gods' undertakings, holding grudges against each other and avenging each others' pranks and misdemeanours, just as humans do; gods whose arrows can be diverted from the intended targets by arrows released from the bows of other similarly divine archers. Gods could sustain their divine authority and keep it unquestioned and uncontested only jointly, as a group, the larger the better – so that the reason for a god or a goddess not having kept their divine promises could always be found in an equally divine curse cast by another of the residents in the crowded Pantheon, and so without a grudge being held against divinity as such, or their summary wisdom being doubted.

All those comfortable explanations of the irritating randomness with which divine grace and condemnation were scattered, a hap-hazardness evidently deaf and immune to human piety or impiety, merits and sins, ceased to be available once the very existence of a Pantheon had been denied and the 'one-and-only' God had laid claim to unshared and indivisible, comprehensive and uncontested rule, decrying thereby all other deities (other tribal gods, or 'partial', 'specialist' gods) as nothing but false pretenders, and bending their efforts to proving their impotence. Taking absolute *power*, full and indivisible sovereignty over the universe, the God of monotheistic religion took absolute *responsibility* for the blessings and blows of fate – for the bad luck of the miserable as much as for the (as Goethe would say) 'long row of sunny days' of those pampered by fortune. Absolute power means *no excuse*. If the caring and protective God has no rivals, neither has He a sensible, let alone obvious, apology for the evils tormenting humans under his rule.

The Book of Job recasts the frightening *randomness* of Nature as the frightening *arbitrariness* of its Ruler. It proclaims that *God does not owe his worshippers account of His actions*, and most certainly *does not owe them an apology*: as Leszek Kołakowski crisply put it, 'God owes us nothing' (neither justice, nor an excuse for its absence). God's omnipotence includes the licence to turn and turn about, to say one thing and do another; it presumes the power of caprice and whim, the power to make miracles and to ignore the logic of necessity which lesser beings have no choice but to obey. God may strike at will, and if He refrains from striking, it is only because this is His (good, benign, benevolent, loving) will. The idea that humans may *control* God's action by whatever means, including the means which God Himself has recommended (that is, total and unconditional submission, a meek and faithful following of His commands and an adherence to the letter of the Divine Law), is a blasphemy.

In stark opposition to the numb and dumb Nature which He rules, incarnates and personifies, God *speaks* and *gives commands*. He also finds out whether the commands have been obeyed, and will reward the obedient and punish the obstreperous. He is *not indifferent* to what human weaklings think and do. But just like numb and dumb Nature, he is *not bound* by what humans think or do. He can *make exceptions* and the logics of consistency and universality are not exempt from exercising that Divine prerogative ('miracle' means in the last resort a violation of a rule, and a departure from consistency and universality). Indeed, the unconditional rule of a norm is by definition irreconcilable with true sovereignty – with the absolute power to *decide*. To be absolute, power must include the right and the ability to neglect, suspend or abolish the norm, that is to commit acts which on the receiving end rebound as miracles. Schmitt's idea of the sovereignty of the ruler would engrave a preformed vision of divine order onto the ground of state legislative order: 'The exception in jurisprudence is analogous to the miracle in theology . . . [T]he legal order rests on a *decision* and not a *norm*.'[1] The power to exempt is the foundation simultaneously of God's absolute power and human beings' continuing, incurable fear born of insecurity – fear that no volume of piety is sufficient to chase away and to bar from returning. And this is exactly what, according to Schmitt, happens in the case of the human sovereign who is no longer handcuffed by norms. Thanks to that power of exemption, humans are, as they were in the times before the Law, vulnerable and uncertain. Only now their fear will not lead to sinful doubt about the sovereign's omnipotence. On the contrary, it will make that omnipotence all the more obvious and commanding.

Which brings us back to the beginning, to the 'cosmic', or *primal*, fear which, according to Mikhail Bakhtin, is the source of religion and politics alike.

Unravelling the mystery of earthly human, all-too-human power, Mikhail Bakhtin, one of the greatest Russian philosophers of the past century, began from a description of 'cosmic fear', the human, all-too-human emotion aroused by the unearthly, inhuman magnificence of the universe; the kind of fear that precedes man-made power and serves as its foundation, prototype and inspiration.[2] *Cosmic* fear, in Bakhtin's words, is the trepidation felt in the face of the immeasurably great and immeasurably powerful: in the face of the starry heavens, the material mass of the mountains, the sea, and the fear of cosmic upheavals and elemental disasters. At the core of 'cosmic fear' lies, let us note, the nonentity of the frightened, wan and transient being faced with the enormity of the everlasting universe; the sheer weakness, incapacity to resist, *vulnerability* of the eminently mortal, frail and soft human body that the sight of the 'starry heavens' or 'the material mass of the mountains' reveals; but also the realization that it is not in human power to grasp, comprehend or mentally assimilate that awesome might manifesting itself in the sheer grandeur of the universe. That universe escapes all understanding. Its intentions are *unknown*, its next doings *unpredictable*, and irresistible even when guessed. If there is a preconceived plan or logic in its doings, it certainly escapes the ability of humans to *comprehend*. And so 'cosmic fear' is also a horror of the unknown and the indomitable: in a nutshell, the terror of *uncertainty*.

Vulnerability and uncertainty are also the two qualities of the human condition out of which that other fear, the 'official fear' – fear of *human* power, of man-*made* and man-*held* power – is moulded. 'Official fear' is construed after the pattern of the inhuman power reflected by (or rather emanating from) 'cosmic fear'.

Bakhtin suggests that cosmic fear is used by all religious systems. The image of God, the supreme ruler of the universe and its inhabitants, is moulded out of the familiar emotion of fear of vulnerability and trembling in the face of impenetrable and irreparable uncertainty. But let us note that when remoulded by a religious doctrine, pristine, primeval cosmic fear undergoes a fateful transformation.

In its original form in which it was spontaneously born, it is a fear of an *anonymous* and *dumb* force. The universe frightens, but does not speak. It demands nothing. It gives no instructions on how to proceed, it could not care less what frightened, vulnerable humans will do or will refrain from doing. It cannot be immolated, flattered or offended. There is no point in talking to the starry heavens, mountains or sea and trying to ingratiate oneself into their favours. They will not hear, and they would not listen if they heard, let alone answer. There is no point in trying to earn their forgiveness or benevolence. Besides, despite all their tremendous might, they could not abide by the penitents' wishes even if they cared about them; they lack not just eyes, ears, minds and hearts, but also the ability to choose and the power of discretion, and so also the ability to act on their will and to accelerate or slow down, arrest or reverse what would have happened anyway. Their moves are inscrutable to human weaklings, but also to themselves. They are, as the biblical God declared at the beginning of his conversation with Moses, 'what they are', full stop – yet *without* declaring even that little.

'I am that I am' were the first recorded words coming from the superhuman source of cosmic fear in that memorable encounter on the top of Mount Sinai. Once those words had been spoken, just *because* there were words spoken, that superhuman source ceased to be anonymous, even though it abstained from introducing itself by name and stayed beyond human control and comprehension. *Humans* remained vulnerable and uncertain as before, and so terrified – but something enormously important happened to the *source* of their cosmic fear: it stopped being deaf and dumb; it acquired control over its own conduct. From now on, it could be benign or cruel, could reward or punish. It could make demands and render its own conduct dependent on whether they were obeyed or not. Not only could it *speak*, but it could be *spoken to*, humoured or angered.

And so, curiously, while reforging frightened beings into slaves of divine commands, that wondrous transformation of the Universe into God was also an act of *oblique human empowerment*. From now on, humans had to be docile, submissive and compliant – but they could also, at least in principle, do something to make sure that the awesome catastrophes they feared would pass them by and the blessing they coveted would come their way. Now they could gain nights free from nightmares and full of hope in exchange for days filled with acquiescence. 'There were thunders and lightnings, and a thick cloud upon the mount . . . and the whole mount quaked greatly' 'so that all the people that was in the camp trembled'. But among all that blood-curdling and mind-boggling turmoil and racket, the voice of God had been heard: 'Now therefore, if ye will obey my voice indeed, and keep my covenant, then ye shall be a particular treasure to me above all people.' 'And all the people answered together, and said, all that the Lord hath spoken we will do' (*Exodus* 19). Obviously pleased with their oath of unswerving obedience, God promised the people to lead them 'onto a land flowing with milk and honey' (*Exodus* 33). God offered his people a covenant: you listen to me and obey, and I'll make you happy. And a covenant is a contract which, once entered, is binding on *both* sides. Or at least this is what it should be and is expected to be.

One can see that if this is meant to be a story of cosmic fear recycled into 'official' fear (as Bakhtin suggested), the story told so far has been unsatisfactory, or perhaps incomplete. It tells us that (and how) people came to be restrained in whatever they did by the code of law (which had been spelled out in meticulous detail after they had signed a blank cheque promising to obey God's wishes whatever those wishes might be); but it suggests as well that God, once transformed as the source of 'official' fear, is to be similarly restrained and bound – by his people's piety. And so, paradoxically, God (or the Nature He stood for) had acquired will and discretion only to surrender them again! By the simple expedient of being *docile*, people could *oblige* God to be benevolent. People thereby acquired a patent (one is tempted to say: foolproof) medicine against vulnerability, and got rid of the spectre of uncertainty, or at least could manage to keep it at a safe distance. Providing they observed the Law to the letter, they would be neither vulnerable nor tormented by uncertainty. But without vulnerability and uncertainty, there would be no fear; and without fear, no power . . . If rule-bound, the omnipotent God risks being a *contradictio in adiecto* – a contradiction in terms – a *powerless* God. But a powerless God is *not* a force on which one can rely to deliver on the promise to make people his 'particular treasure' 'above all people'. It was that paradox which the Book of Job undertook to resolve.

While blatantly violating the rulings of God's covenant with His 'particular treasure' one by one, the *story* of Job was all but incomprehensible to the denizens of a modern state conceived as a *Rechtstaat*. It went against the grain of what they had been trained to believe the meaning of the contractual obligations by which their life was guided, and so also the harmony and logic of civilized life, were about. To philosophers, the story of Job was a continuous and incurable headache; it dashed their hopes of discovering, or of instilling, logic and harmony in the chaotic flow of events called 'history'. Generations of theologians broke their teeth, trying in vain to bite at its mystery: like the rest of modern men and women (and everyone who memorized the message of the Book of Exodus), they had been taught to seek a rule and a norm, but the message of the book was that there was no rule and no norm to be relied upon; more exactly, no rule or norm that the supreme power is bound by. The Book of Job anticipates the blunt verdict of Carl Schmitt that 'the sovereign is he who has the power of exemption'. Power to impose rules stems from the power to suspend them or make null and void.

Carl Schmitt, arguably the most clear-headed, illusion-free anatomist of the modern state and its in-built totalitarian inclinations, avers: 'He who determines a value, *eo ipso* always fixes a nonvalue. The sense of this determination of a nonvalue is the annihilation of the nonvalue.'[3] Determining the value draws the limits of the normal, the ordinary, the orderly. Nonvalue is an exception that marks this boundary.

> *The exception is that which cannot be subsumed*; it defies general codification, but it simultaneously reveals a specifically juridical formal element: the decision in absolute purity [. . .] There is no rule that is applicable to chaos. Order must be established for juridical order to make sense. A regular situation must be created, and *sovereign is he who definitely decides if this situation is actually effective* . . . The exception not only confirms the rule; the rule as such lives off the exception alone.[4]

Giorgio Agamben, the brilliant Italian philosopher, comments:

> *The rule applies to the exception in no longer applying, in withdrawing from it.* The state of exception is thus not a simple return to the chaos that preceded order but rather the situation that results from its suspension. In this sense, the exception is truly, according to its etymological root, *taken outside* [*ex-capere*], and not simply excluded.[5]

In other words, there is no contradiction between *establishing a rule* and *making an exception*. Quite the contrary: without the power to exempt from the rule, there would be no power to make the rule stand . . .

All this is admittedly confusing; it may defy commonsense logic, yet this is the truth of *power*, and it has to be reckoned with in any attempt to comprehend its works. Understanding is at cross-purposes with believing: it makes belief conditional on the logic-ruled comprehension, and therefore perpetually provisional. Only the incomprehensible can be unconditionally believed. Without the Book of Job, the Book of Exodus would fail to lay the foundations for God's omnipotence and Israel's obedience.

The story of Job's life told in that Book was the most acute and insidious (and the least easy to repel) of conceivable challenges to the idea of order resting on a universal norm instead of on (arbitrary) decisions. Given the contents of the toolbox and the routines currently available to reason, Job's life story was a gauntlet thrown down to the very possibility of the creatures who were endowed with reason, and therefore yearning for logic, feeling at home in the world. Just as the ancient astronomers went on desperately drawing ever new epicycles to defend the geocentric world order against the unruly evidence of the sightings in the night sky, the learned theologians quoted in the Book of Job leaned over backwards to defend the unbreakability of the links between sin and punishment and virtue and reward against the evidence being steadily supplied of the pains inflicted on Job – in every respect an exemplary person, a God-fearing, pious creature, a true paragon of virtue. As if it was not enough that there had been a resounding failure to advance clinching proof that the credibility of routine explanations of evil had emerged unscathed from the acid test of pious Job's misfortune, the dense fog in which the allocation of good and bad luck was closely wrapped did not disperse when God himself joined the debate . . .

When Job begged: 'Tell me plainly, and I will listen in silence: show me where I have erred . . . Why hast thou made me thy butt, and why have I become thy target?' (Job 6: 24; 7: 20), he waited in vain for God's answer. Job expected as much: 'Indeed this I know for the truth, that no man can win his case against God. If a man chooses to argue with him, God will not answer one question in a thousand . . . Though I am right, I get no answer . . . Blameless, I say . . . But it is all one; therefore I say: He destroys blameless and wicked alike' (Job 9: 2–3; 9: 15, 22).

Job expected no answer to his complaint, and at least on this point he was evidently in the right. God ignored his question, and questioned instead Job's right to ask: 'Brace yourself and stand like a man; I will ask questions, and you shall answer. Dare you deny that I am just or put me in the wrong that you may be right? Have you an arm like God's arm, can you thunder with a voice like his?' (Job 40: 6–9). God's questions were only rhetorical, of course; Job knew only too well that he had no arm or voice to match God's, and so by implication he was aware that it was not God who owed him an explanation but he who owed God an apology. (Let's note that, on the authority of Holy Scripture, it was God's questions, not Job's, that came 'out of the tempest' – that archetype of all other blows known to be deaf to pleas for mercy and to strike at random . . .)

What Job might have been as yet unaware of was that in the centuries to come all the earthly pretenders to God-like omnipotence would find the unpredictability and haphazardness of their thundering to be the most awesome of their weapons by far, the most terrorizing and invincible. Anyone who wished to steal the rulers' thunders would first have to disperse the fog of uncertainty wrapped around them and recast *randomness* into *regularity*, the state of 'anomie' (*normlessness*, or a fluidity of the limits to normative regulation) into *norm*. But then Job could not anticipate that; he was not a creature of modernity.

Susan Neiman and Jean-Pierre Dupuy have recently suggested that the earthquake, fire and high tide that jointly, in quick succession, destroyed Lisbon in 1755 marked the beginning of the modern philosophy of evil.[6] Modern philosophers set *natural* disasters apart from *moral* evils, the difference being precisely the *randomness* of the first (now recast as blindness) and the *intentionality* or *purposefulness* of the second.

Neiman points out that 'since Lisbon, natural evils no longer have any seemly relations to moral evils, since they no longer have meaning at all' (Husserl suggested that *Meinung* – 'meaning' – comes from *meinen,* 'intending'; later, post-Husserl, generations of philosophers would take it for granted that there is no meaning without intention). Lisbon was like a stage production of the story of Job, performed on the Atlantic coast in the full glare of publicity and in the view of all Europe – though, this time, God, His prerogatives and credentials, were to be largely absent from the dispute that followed the event.

True to the nature of all disputes, the standpoints of the discussants differed. According to Dupuy, the protagonist who struck the most modern chord in the debate was paradoxically Jean-Jacques Rousseau, who, because of his celebration of the pristine wisdom of everything 'natural', was all too often mistaken for a hopelessly pre- and anti-modern thinker. In his open letter to Voltaire, Rousseau insisted that the fault, if not for the Lisbon disaster itself, then most certainly for its catastrophic consequences and their horrifying scale, belonged to human beings not to nature (note: *fault*, not *sin* – unlike God, Nature had no faculties for judging the moral quality of human deeds). It was the outcome of human myopia, not nature's blindness; a product of mundane human greed, not nature's lofty indifference. If only 'the residents of that large city had been dispersed more evenly, and built lighter houses, there would have been much less damage, perhaps even none at all . . . And how many wretches lost their lives in the catastrophe because they wished to collect their belongings – some their papers, some others their money?'[7]

In the long run at least, Rousseau-style arguments came out on top. Modern philosophy followed the pattern set by Pombal, the prime minister of Portugal at the time of the Lisbon catastrophe, whose concerns and actions 'focused on eradicating those evils that *could be reached by human hands*'.[8] And let's add that modern philosophers expected, hoped and believed that human hands, once they were equipped with scientifically designed and technologically supplied extensions, would be able to stretch further – eventually far enough to handle whatever was needed. They trusted that as human hands lengthened, the number of evils remaining outside their reach would fall; even to zero, given enough time and sufficient resolve.

Two and a half centuries later we can opine, however, that what the philosophical and non-philosophizing pioneers of modernity expected to happen was not to be. As Neiman sums up the lessons of the two centuries separating Lisbon, that trigger of modern ambitions, from Auschwitz, that collapsed them:

> Lisbon revealed how remote the world is from humans; Auschwitz revealed the remoteness of humans from themselves. If disentangling the natural from the human is part of the modern project, the distance between Lisbon and Auschwitz showed how difficult it was to keep them apart . . . If Lisbon marked the moment of recognition that traditional theodicy was hopeless, Auschwitz signalled the recognition that every replacement fared no better.[9]

As long as it confronted humans in the guise of an omnipotent yet benevolent God, nature was a mystery that defied human comprehension: how, indeed, to square God's benevolence cum omnipotence with the profusion of evil in a world which He himself had designed and set in motion? The solutions to that quandary most commonly on offer – that the natural disasters visited upon humanity were so many just punishments visited upon moral sinners by God, that supreme ethical legislature, supreme court of justice and executive arm of moral law rolled into one – did not account for the stark evidence, summarized laconically by Voltaire in his poem composed to commemorate the 1755 Lisbon earthquake and fire: 'l'innocent, ainsi que le coupable, / subit également ce mal inévitable'.[10] The mind-boggling quandary haunted the Philosophes of emergent modernity just as it did generations of theologians. The evident profligacy of evil in the world could not be reconciled with the combination of benevolence and omnipotence imputed to the world's maker and supreme manager.

The contradiction could not be resolved; it could only be taken off the agenda by what Max Weber described as the *Entzäuberung* ('disenchantment') of nature, which means derobing nature of its divine disguise – chosen as the true birth-act of the 'modern spirit': that is, of the hubris grounded in the new 'we can do it, we will do it' attitude of self-assurance and confidence. In a sort of penalty for the inefficacy of obedience, prayer and the practice of virtue (the three instruments recommended as a sure way to evoke desirable responses from the benevolent and omnipotent Divine Subject), nature was stripped of subjecthood, and so denied the very *capacity* of choosing between its own benevolence and malice. Humans could hope to ingratiate themselves in God's eyes and could even protest God's verdicts and argue and negotiate their cases, but trying to debate and bargain with 'disenchanted' nature in the hope of currying grace was evidently pointless. Nature had been stripped of subjectivity not in order to restore and salvage the subjectivity of God, however, but to pave the way to a *deification of His human subjects*.

With human beings put in charge, uncertainty and uncertainty-fed 'cosmic fears' did not vanish, of course, and Nature stripped of its Divine disguise appeared no less tremendous, menacing and terror-inspiring than before; but what the prayers failed to accomplish, science-supported *techne*, targeted at dealing with blind and *dumb* nature though not with an omniscient and *speaking* God, surely would, once it had accumulated the skills to do things and used them to have things done. One could now expect the randomness and unpredictability of nature to be only a temporary irritant, and believe the prospect of forcing nature into obedience to the human will to be but a matter of time. *Natural* disasters might (and should!) be subjected to the same treatment as that designed for *social* ills, the kinds of adversities that, with due skill and effort, could be exiled from the human world and barred from returning. The discomforts caused by nature's antics would eventually be dealt with as effectively, at least in principle, as the calamities brought about by human malice and wantonness. Sooner or later, *all* threats, natural and moral alike, would become predictable and preventable, obedient to the power of reason. How soon it would happen depended solely on the determination with which the powers of human reason were deployed. Nature would become just like those other aspects of the human condition that are evidently made by humans and so in principle manageable and 'correctible'. As Immanuel Kant's categorical imperative implied, when we deploy reason, our inalienable endowment, we can raise the moral judgement and the kind of behaviour we wish to be universally followed to the rank of *natural law*.

This is how it was *hoped* human affairs would develop at the start of the modern era and through a good part of its history. As present experience suggests, however, they *have been* developing in the opposite direction. Rather than reason-guided behaviour being *promoted* to the rank of natural law, its consequences were *degraded* to the level of irrational nature. Natural catastrophes did not become more like 'in principle manageable' moral misdeeds; on the contrary, it was the lot of immorality to become or be revealed as ever more similar to the 'classic' natural catastrophes: hazardous like them, unpredictable, unpreventable, incomprehensible and immune to human reason and wishes. Disasters brought about by human action nowadays arrive from an opaque world, strike at random, in places impossible to anticipate, and escape or defy the kind of explanation that sets human actions apart from all other events: an explanation by *motive* or *purpose*. Above all, the calamities caused by human immoral actions appear ever more unmanageable *in principle*.

This is what Carl Schmitt found in the world he was born into and grew up in. A world divided between secular states which, according to a retrospective summary scripted by Ernst-Wolfgang Böckenförde, 'lived off preconditions they could not themselves guarantee'.[11] The modern vision of a 'powerful, rational state', a 'state of real substance', 'standing above society and remaining immune from sectarian interests',[12] a state capable of claiming the standing of the precondition or determinant of social order, a standing once held but now relinquished by God, seemed to dissolve and evaporate in the reality of sectarian strife, revolutions, powers incapable of acting and societies reluctant to be acted upon.

The ideas that assisted at the birth of the modern era hoped and promised to eliminate and extirpate once and for all the erratic twists and turns of contingent fate, together with the resulting opacity and unpredictability of the human condition and prospects that marked the rule of the Jerusalem God: these ideas 'rejected the exception in every form'.[13] They sought an alternative, solid and reliable precondition of social order in the constitutional liberal state, expected to replace the capricious finger of divine providence with the invisible, yet steady hand of the market. Such hopes have abominably failed to be fulfilled, whereas the promises turned out to hang anywhere except within the reach of the states they envisaged. In his garb of the modern 'powerful and rational' state, the Jerusalem God found himself in Athens, that messy playground of mischievous and scheming gods – where, to follow Plato, the other gods would die of laughter when they heard his pretence to the status of the 'one and only', while (to be on the safe side) making sure that their quivers were full of arrows.

As long as the theorists and panegyrists of the modern state followed the lead of the Jerusalem God who stoutly refused to recognize other pretenders to divine status, the pages of the Book of Job were obviously missing from their gospels. The reconciliation of happy-go-lucky Athenians to the plurality of obstreperously uncomplaisant and quarrelsome gods (the kind of settlement brought to its logical conclusion by the Roman practice of adding new busts to the Pantheon with every new territorial conquest) would not do for the hapless residents of the modern world, that precarious arrangement founded on the (un)holy triune alliance between state, nation, and territory.

In this modern world there might be many divinities, as in Athens or Rome, but the places where they could meet and fraternize in peace, such as the Areopagus or the Pantheon designed for their affable conviviality, were missing. Their encounters would make any site into a battlefield and a frontline, since, following the line originated by the Jerusalem God, each triune formation would claim an absolute, inalienable and indivisible sovereignty in its own domain. The world into which Schmitt was born was not the polytheistic world of Athenians or Romans, but a world of *cuius regio eius religio*, of an uneasy cohabitation of viciously competitive, intolerant, self-proclaimed 'one and only' gods. The world populated by states-in-search-of nations and nations-in-search-of states could be (and was likely to remain for still some time) *polytheistic*, but each part of it defended tooth and nail its own prerogative to (religious, secular, or both – as in the case of modern nationalism) *monotheism*. That principle and that intention were to be recorded in the statutes of the League of Nations and restated, with yet greater emphasis, in the rules and regulations of the United Nations, instructed to uphold with all its (genuine or putative) powers the sacrosanct right of every member state to its own uncompromising sovereignty over the fate and lives of its subjects at home. The League of Nations, and later the United Nations, wanted to pull the nation-states bent on sovereignty away from the battlefield, their hitherto normal and tested ground of cohabitation and reciprocal genocide, and sit them instead at a round table, keeping them there and prompting them to converse; it intended to allure the warring tribes to Athens with the promise of making their tribal, Jerusalem-style gods yet more secure – each one in his tribe.

Carl Schmitt saw through the futility of that intention. The charges that can (and should) be laid against him is the charge of liking what he saw, the yet more serious charge of embracing it enthusiastically, and the truly unforgivable charge of earnestly trying to do his best to raise the pattern he distilled from the practices of the twentieth-century Europe to the rank of the eternal law of all and any politics; the charge of conferring on that pattern the distinction of the one and only attribute of a political process that elides and transcends the sovereign's power of exemption and sets a limit to the sovereign's power of decision that he can ignore only at his own mortal peril. A charge of imperfect vision aimed at Schmitt would be groundless, however; it ought to be laid instead at the door of those who saw otherwise and whose vision Schmitt set about correcting.

If you put together Schmitt's assertion that he is sovereign 'who decides on the exception' (more importantly, decides *arbitrarily* – 'decisionistic and personalistic elements' being most crucial in the concept of sovereignty),[14] and his insistence that the distinction defining 'the political' aspect in actions and motives 'is that between friend and enemy',[15] in opposition to which they can be reduced, what follows is that the substance and trademark of all and any holder of sovereignty, and of all and any sovereign agency, is 'association and dissociation'; more exactly, *association-through-dissociation*, deployment of 'dissociation' in the production and servicing of 'association' – naming the enemy that needs to be 'dissociated' so that the friends may remain 'associated'. In a nutshell, pinpointing, setting apart, labelling and declaring war on an enemy. In Schmitt's vision of sovereignty, association is inconceivable without dissociation, order without expulsion and extinction, creation without destruction. The strategy of destruction for the sake of order-building is the defining feature of sovereignty.

The naming of an enemy is 'decisionistic' and 'personalistic' since 'the political enemy need not be morally evil or aesthetically ugly' – indeed, he need not be guilty of hostile deeds or intentions; it is sufficient that 'he is the other, the stranger, something different and alien'.[16] But then, given the decisionistic nature of sovereignty, it must be clear that someone becomes 'the other' and 'the stranger', and ultimately 'an enemy', at *the end*, not the *starting point* of the political action defined as the enemy-naming act and the enemy-fighting action. Indeed, an 'objectivity' of enmity, with the condition of 'being an enemy' being determined by the enemy's own attributes and actions, would go against the grain of a sovereignty that consists in the right to make exceptions; it would be not unlike a covenant equally binding on Jahve and the people of Israel, a settlement unacceptable to modern sovereigns as much as it was to the jealous and vengeful God of the Book of Job. Just as it was Jahve and only Jahve who decided that Job was to be tortured, it is the sovereign at the helm of the state and only he who decides who is to be exempted from law and destroyed. At least, *also sprach Carl Schmitt*, after taking a close look at the practices of the most decisive and unscrupulous seekers of sovereignty of his time; perhaps also after noticing the 'totalitarian inclination' endemic, as Hannah Arendt suggested, to all modern forms of state power.

One of the patients in Alexander Solzhenitsyn's *Cancer Ward* is a local party dignitary who starts every day by attentively reading the editorial in *Pravda*. He is waiting for an operation and his chances of survival are in the balance – and yet, each day, from the moment the new issue of *Pravda* and its new editorial is delivered to the ward, he has no reason to worry; until the next issue arrives, he knows exactly what to do, what to say and how to say it and on what topics to keep silent. In the most important matters, in the choices that truly count, he has the comfort of certainty: he cannot err.

Pravda editorials were notorious for changing their tune from one day to the next. Names and tasks that only yesterday were on everybody's lips might become unmentionable overnight. Deeds or turns of phrase that were right and proper the day before might turn into wrong and abominable ones the day after, while acts unthinkable yesterday might become obligatory today. But under Stalin's decisionistic and personalistic rule, there was no moment, however brief, when the difference between right and wrong, the obligatory and the prohibited, was unclear. So long as you listened and followed what you heard, you couldn't make a mistake; because, as Ludwig Wittgenstein pointed out, 'to understand' means to know how to go on – you were safe, protected against fatal misunderstanding. And your safety was the gift of the Party, and of Stalin, its leader and your unerring guide (it was in his name, surely, that *Pravda* editorials spoke). Telling you each day what to do, Stalin took responsibility off your shoulders by tackling for you the worrisome task of understanding. He was, indeed, *omniscient*. Not necessarily in the sense of knowing everything there was to be known, but of telling you everything that you needed to and should know. Not necessarily in the sense of unerringly distinguishing between truth and error, but of drawing the authoritative boundary between the truth and error that you needed to observe.

In Chiaureli's film *The Oath*, the central character – a Russian Mother, the epitome of the whole gallantly fighting, hardworking and always Stalin-loving and loved-by-Stalin Russian nation – visits Stalin one day and asks him to end the war. The Russian people have suffered so much, she says, they have borne such horrible sacrifices, so many wives have lost their husbands, so many children have lost their fathers – there must be an end to all that pain. Stalin answers: yes, Mother, the time has come to end the war. And he ends the war.

Stalin was not just omniscient, he was also *omnipotent*. If he wanted to end the war, he did. If he did not do what the nation wished him or even asked him to do, it was not for his lack of power or the know-how to oblige, but because there must have been some important reason to postpone the action or refrain from it altogether (it was he, after all, who drew the authoritative boundary between right and wrong). You could be sure that if doing it were a good idea, it would have been done. You yourself, you might be too inept to spot, list and calculate all the pros and cons of the matter, but Stalin protected you against the terrible consequences of miscalculation arising from your ignorance. And so it did not matter in the end that the meaning of what was going on and its logic escaped you and 'others like you'. What might have looked to you like a hotchpotch of uncoordinated events, accidents and random happenings had a logic, a design, a plan, a consistency. The fact that you couldn't see that consistency with your own eyes was one more proof (perhaps the sole proof you needed) of just how crucial to your security the perspicacity of Stalin was and how much you owed to his wisdom and his willingness to share its fruits with you.

Between themselves, the two stories go a long way towards revealing the secret of Stalin's power over the minds and hearts of his subjects. But not far enough . . .

The big question, not only unanswered but unasked, is why the subjects' need of reassurance was so overwhelming that they were prompted to sacrifice their minds for its sake and fill their hearts with gratitude when their sacrifice was accepted. For certainty to have become the supreme need, desire and dream, it must first have been *missing*. As yet unacquired, lost, or stolen.

True to the nature of Schmitt's sovereign, Stalin repeatedly demonstrated his power to launch purges and witch-hunts and to stop or suspend them as abruptly and inexplicably as they had been started. There was no telling which activity will be the next to be stigmatized as witchcraft; and since blows fell at random, and the material proof of any connection with the variety of witchcraft currently being hunted was a frowned-upon luxury, if not a dangerous step obliquely recalling 'objectivity' from its exile, there was no telling either whether there was any intelligible link between what individuals did and the lot they suffered. (This was expressed by Soviet popular wit in the story of the hare who ran for shelter when it heard that camels were being arrested: they'll arrest you first, and then you have to try to prove that you are not a camel . . .) Indeed, nowhere else and at no other time has there been such a profuse and convincing demonstration of the credibility of Calvin's image of a Supreme Being (undoubtedly Schmitt's inspiration) who distributes grace and condemnation by his own inscrutable choice regardless of their targets' conduct, and suffers no appeal or petition against His verdicts.

When everyone, at all times, is vulnerable because of his or her ignorance of what the next morning may bring, it is survival and safety, not a sudden catastrophe, that appears to be the exception, indeed, a miracle that defies an ordinary human being's comprehension and requires superhuman foresight, wisdom and powers to act to be performed. On a scale seldom matched elsewhere, Stalin practised the sovereign power of exemption from the treatment owed by right to legal subjects, or, indeed, to humans for being human. But he also managed to reverse appearances: as the exemptions (the suspension or cancellation of rights, assignments to Giorgio Agamben's *homini sacri*) turned from an exception into a norm, *it was avoidance of the randomly distributed blows that appeared to be an exemption*, an exceptional gift, a show of grace. One should be grateful for the favours one receives. And one was.

Human vulnerability and uncertainty is the foundation of all political power. Powers claim authority and obedience by promising their subjects effective protection against these two banes of the human condition. In the Stalinist variety of totalitarian power, that is in the absence of the randomness of the human condition produced by the market, vulnerability and uncertainty had to be produced and reproduced by the political power itself. It was more than sheer coincidence that random terror was unleashed on a massive scale at a time when the last residues of NEP – the 'New Economic Policy' inviting the market back in after its banishment in the years of 'war communism' – were dismantled.

In most modern societies, the vulnerability and insecurity of existence and the need to pursue one's life purposes under conditions of acute and unredeemable uncertainty was assured from the start by the exposure of life pursuits to the vagaries of market forces. Apart from protecting market freedoms and occasionally helping to resuscitate the dwindling vigour of market forces, political power had no need to interfere. In demanding its subjects' discipline and observance of law, it could rest its legitimacy on the promise to mitigate the extent of the already existing vulnerability and uncertainty of its citizens: to limit the harms and damages perpetrated by the free play of market forces, to shield the vulnerable against mortal or excessively painful blows, and to insure against at least some risks among the many which free competition necessarily entails. Such legitimation found its ultimate expression in the self-definition of the modern form of government as a 'welfare state'.

That formula of political power is presently receding into the past. 'Welfare state' institutions are progressively being dismantled and phased out, while restraints previously imposed on business activities and on the free play of market competition and its dire consequences are being removed one by one. The protective functions of the state are being tapered to embrace a small minority who are unemployable and invalid, though even that minority tends to be reclassified from the 'issue of social care' into an 'issue of law and order': an incapacity to participate in the market game tends increasingly to be criminalized. The state is washing its hands of the vulnerability and uncertainty arising from the logic (or illogic) of the free market, redefining them as a private fault and a private affair, a matter for individuals to deal with and cope with through the resources in their private possession. As Ulrich Beck put it, individuals are now expected to seek biographical solutions to systemic contradictions.[17]

These new trends have a side-effect: they sap the foundations on which state power, claiming a crucial role in fighting the vulnerability and uncertainty haunting its subjects, increasingly rested in modern times. The widely noted growth of political apathy, the erosion of political interests and loyalties ('no more salvation by society', as Peter Drucker famously put it, or 'there is no society; there are only individuals and the families', as Margaret Thatcher equally bluntly declared), and a massive retreat of the population from participation in institutionalized politics, all testify to the crumbling of the established foundations of state power.

Having rescinded its previous programmatic interference with market-produced insecurity, and having on the contrary proclaimed the perpetuation and intensification of that insecurity to be the mission of all political power caring for the well-being of its subjects, the contemporary state must seek other, non-economic varieties of vulnerability and uncertainty on which to rest its legitimacy. That alternative seems to have been recently located (perhaps most spectacularly, but by no means exclusively, by the United States administration) in the issue of personal safety: threats to human bodies, possessions and habitats arising from criminal activities, anti-social conduct by the 'underclass', and most recently global terrorism and, increasingly, 'illegitimate immigrants'. Unlike the insecurity born of the market, which is if anything all too visible and obvious for comfort, that alternative insecurity with which the state hopes to restore its lost monopoly of redemption must be artificially beefed up, or at least highly dramatized to inspire sufficient 'official fear' and at the same time overshadow and relegate to a secondary position the economically generated insecurity about which the state administration can do – and wishes to do – nothing. Unlike the market-generated threats to social standing, self-worth and livelihood, the extent of the dangers to personal safety must be presented in the darkest of colours, so that (much as under the Stalinist political regime) the *non-materialization of threats* can be applauded as an extra-ordinary event, a result of the vigilance, care and good will of state organs. *No wonder the power of exemption, states of emergency and the appointment of enemies are having a heyday.* It is a moot question whether the power to exempt is an eternal essence of all sovereignty, and whether the selection and pillorying of enemies is the extemporal substance of 'the political'; there is little doubt, however, that nowadays the muscles of the powers that be are being flexed in the pursuit of these two activities as hardly ever before.

These are the activities with which the Central Intelligence Agency and the Federal Bureau of Investigation have been most occupied in recent years: warning Americans of imminent attempts on their safety, putting them in a state of constant alert and so building up tension – so that there is tension to be relieved when the attempts do not occur and so that all the credit for its relief can, by popular consent, be ascribed to the organs of law and order to which state administration is progressively reduced.

On 10 June 2002 US officials of the highest rank (FBI Director Robert Mueller, US Deputy Attorney General Larry Thompson, Deputy Defense Secretary Paul Wolfowitz among others) announced the arrest of a suspected al-Qaeda terrorist on his return to Chicago from a training trip to Pakistan.[18] As the official version of the affair claimed, an American citizen, American born and bred, José Padilla (the name suggests Hispanic roots, that is, one of the latest, relatively poorly settled, additions to the long list of immigrant ethnic affiliations) converted to Islam, took the name of Abdullah al-Muhajir, and promptly went to his new Muslim brethren for instructions on how to harm his erstwhile homeland. He was instructed in the artless art of patching together 'dirty bombs' – 'frighteningly easy to assemble' out of a few ounces of widely available conventional explosives and 'virtually any type of radioactive material' that the would-be terrorists 'can get their hands on' (it was not clear why sophisticated training was needed to assemble weapons 'frighteningly easy to assemble', but when it comes to the use of diffuse fears as a fertilizer for the grapes of wrath, logic is neither here nor there). 'A new phrase entered the post-Sept. 11 vocabulary of many average Americans: dirty bomb,' announced *USA Today* reporters Nichols, Hall and Eisler.

As it became clear in the years that followed, this was only the humble beginning of a powerful and overwhelming trend. On the last day of 2007 the *New York Times* ran an editorial insisting that the United States could hardly be described any longer as a 'democratic society'. The editorial enumerated a list of state-sanctioned abuses, including torture by the CIA and subsequent repeated violations of the Geneva Conventions, a web of legalized illegality enabling the Bush administration to spy on Americans, and a willingness of government officials to violate civil and constitutional rights without apology, all done under the aegis of conducting a war on terrorism. The editorial board of the *New York Times* argued that since 11 September 2001 the United States government had induced a 'state of lawless behaviour'. The *New York Times* was not the only one voicing such concerns. The prominent writer, Sidney Blumenthal, a former senior adviser to President Clinton, claimed that Americans were now living under a government tantamount to 'a national security state of torture, ghost detainees, secret prisons, renditions and domestic eavesdropping'.[19] Bob Herbert, an op-ed writer for the *New York Times*, argued that the dark landscapes of exclusion, secrecy, illegal surveillance and torture produced under the Bush regime offered Americans nothing less than a 'road map to totalitarianism'.[20]

As Henry A. Giroux has recently pointed out, however,

it is a mistake to suggest that the Bush administration is solely responsible for transforming the United States to the degree that it has now become unrecognizable to itself as a democratic nation. Such claims risk reducing the serious social ills now plaguing the United States to the reactionary policies of the Bush regime – a move which allows for complacency to set in as Bush's reign comes to a close on January 20, 2009. The complacency caused by the sense of immanent regime change fails to offer a truly political response to the current crisis because it ignores the extent to which Bush's policies merely recapitulate Clinton era social and economic policy. Actually, what the United States has become in the last decade suggests less of a rupture than an intensification of a number of underlying political, economic, and social forces that have ushered in a new era in which the repressive anti-democratic tendencies lurking beneath the damaged heritage of democratic ideals have now emerged swiftly and forcefully as the new face of a deeply disturbing authoritarianism. What marks the present state of American 'democracy' is the uniquely bipolar nature of the degenerative assault on the body politic, which combines elements of unprecedented greed and fanatical capitalism, called by some the New Gilded Age, with a new kind of politics more ruthless and savage in its willingness to abandon – even vilify – those individuals and groups now rendered disposable within 'new geographies of exclusion and landscapes of wealth' that mark the new world order.[21]

All this happened in the USA; but similar efforts to increase the volume of fear and provide the targets on which to unload the resulting anxiety is noticeable worldwide. Donald G. McNeil Jr fitted his summary of the most recent shifts in the European political spectrum: 'Politicians pander to fear of crime'.[22] Indeed, throughout the world ruled by democratically elected governments, 'I'll be tough on crime' has turned out to be the trump card that beats all others, but the winning hand is almost invariably a combination of a promise of 'more prisons, more policemen, longer sentences' with an oath of 'no immigration, no asylum rights, no naturalization'. As McNeil put it, 'Politicians across Europe use the "outsiders cause crime" stereotype to link ethnic hatred, which is unfashionable, to the more palatable fear for one's own safety'. Obviously, politicians all over Europe would not need to play second fiddle to the American tune-setters and scriptwriters.

Vainly trying to escape Nazi-dominated Europe, Walter Benjamin noted that legal exception and legal norm had exchanged places, that the state of exception had become a rule.[23] A little more than half a century later, in his study of the historical antecedents of the state of emergency,[24] Giorgio Agamben came to the conclusion that the state of exception (whether referred to by the names of 'state of emergency', 'state of siege', or 'martial law') 'tends increasingly to appear as the dominant paradigm of government in contemporary politics'. Ever more profuse laws, decrees and orders tend to 'radically erase any legal status of the individual, thus producing a legally unnameable and unclassifiable being'.

Stalin's way of deploying 'official fear' in the service of state power is, we may hope, in the past. This cannot be said, though, about the issue itself. Fifty years after Stalin's death, it arises daily on the agenda of modern powers desperately seeking new and improved forms of its employment to close the gap left by the enforced, but also eagerly pursued, renunciation of their original formula for self-legitimation. The secret of sovereignty laid bare by Carl Schmitt may be extemporal, but the ever more frequent resort to the prerogatives of exemption has its time-bound historical causes. And, hopefully, historically bound duration.

9

A natural history of evil

It is highly unlikely that a twenty-first-century reader of Anatole France's novel *Les Dieux ont soif*, originally published in 1912,[1] won't be simultaneously bewildered and enraptured. In all likelihood, they will be overwhelmed, as I have been, with admiration for an author who not only, as Milan Kundera would say, managed to 'tear through the curtain of preinterpretations', the 'curtain hanging in front of the world', in order to free 'the great human conflicts from naïve interpretation as a struggle between good and evil, understanding them in the light of tragedy'[2] – which in Kundera's opinion is the calling of novelists and the vocation of all novel-writing – but in addition designed and tested, for the benefit of his readers of the future, as yet unborn, the tools with which to cut and tear the curtains not yet woven, but certain to start being eagerly woven and hung 'in front of the world' well after his novel was finished, and particularly eagerly well after his death . . .

At the moment Anatole France put aside his pen and took one last look at his finished novel, there were no words like 'bolshevism', 'fascism', or indeed 'totalitarianism', listed in dictionaries, French or any other; and no names like Stalin or Hitler in any of the history books. Anatole France's attention was focused on Evariste Gamelin, a juvenile beginner in the world of fine art, a youngster of great talent and promise, but possessing yet greater disgust for Watteau, Boucher, Fragonard and other dictators of popular taste, whose 'bad taste, bad drawings, bad designs', 'complete absence of clear style and clear line', 'complete unawareness of nature and truth' and fondness for 'masks, dolls, fripperies, childish nonsense' he explained by their readiness to 'work for tyrants and slaves'. Gamelin was sure that 'a hundred years hence all Watteau's paintings will have rotted away in attics' and predicted that 'by 1893 art students will be covering the canvases of Boucher with their own rough sketches'. The French Republic, still a tender, unsound and frail child of the Revolution, would grow to cut off, one after the other, the many heads of the hydra of tyranny and slavery, including the dearth of artists' clear style and their blindness to Nature. There is no mercy for the conspirators against the Republic, as there is no liberty for the enemies of liberty, nor tolerance for the enemies of tolerance. To the doubts voiced by his incredulous mother, Gamelin would respond without hesitation: 'We must put our trust in Robespierre; he is incorruptible. Above all, we must trust in Marat. He is the one who really loves the people, who realizes their true interests and serves them. He was always the first to unmask the traitors and frustrate plots.' In one of his few and far between authorial interventions, France explains and brands the thoughts and deeds of his hero and his hero's likes as the 'serene fanaticism' of 'little men, who had demolished the throne itself and turned upside down the old order of things'. On his own way from the youth of a Romanian fascist to the adulthood of a French philosopher, Émile Cioran summed up the lot of youngsters of the era of Robespierre and Marat, and Stalin and Hitler alike: 'Bad luck is their lot. It is they who voice the doctrine of intolerance and it is they who put that doctrine into practice. It is they who are thirsty – for blood, tumult, barbarity.'[3] Well, all the youngsters? And only the youngsters? And only in the eras of Robespierre or Stalin?

For Kant, respect and goodwill for others is an imperative of reason; which means that if a human being, a creature endowed by God or Nature with reason, ponders on Kant's reasoning, she or he will surely recognize and accept the categorical character of that imperative and will adopt it as a precept of her or his conduct. In its essence, the categorical imperative in question boils down to the commandment to treat others as you would wish to be treated by them; in other words, to another version of the biblical injunction to love your neighbour as yourself – only in the Kantian case grounded on an elaborate and refined series of logical arguments, and thus invoking the authority of *human reason* as able to judge what needs to be and must be, instead of the *will of God* deciding what ought to be.

In such a translation from sacred to secular language something of the commandment's persuasive powers is lost, however. The will of God, unashamedly 'decisionist', can *bestow* apodictic, unquestionable power on the presumption of an essential, preordained and inescapable symmetry of interhuman relations, a presumption indispensable for both the sacred and the secular versions; whereas reason would have a lot of trouble *demonstrating* that presumption's veracity. The assertion of the symmetry of interhuman relations belongs, after all, in the universe of beliefs, of what is taken for granted or stipulated (and may therefore be accepted on the grounds of 'if would be better, if . . .' or 'we owe obedience to God's will'); but it has no place in the universe of empirically testable knowledge – that domain, or rather the natural habitat, of reason. Whether the advocates of the legislative powers of reason refer to reason's infallibility in its search for truth (for 'how things indeed are and cannot but be'), or to reason's utilitarian merits (that is, its ability to separate realistic, feasible and plausible intentions from mere daydreaming), they will find it difficult to argue convincingly for the reality of symmetry, and still more difficult to prove the usefulness of practising it.

The problem is the paucity, to say the least, of experiential evidence supporting the debated presumption, whereas reason rests its claim to the last word where there is contention on its resolution to ground its judgements precisely in that kind of evidence, while dismissing the validity of all other grounds. Another, yet closely related problem is the profusion of contrary evidence: namely, that when promoting the effectiveness of human undertakings and humans' dexterity in reaching their objectives, reason focuses on liberating its carriers from constraints imposed on their choices by symmetry, mutuality, reversibility of actions and obligations; in other words, on creating situations in which the carriers of reason may quietly strike off the list of factors relevant to their choices the apprehension that the course of action they take may rebound on them – or, to put it brutally, yet more to the point, that evil may boomerang back on the evildoers. Contrary to Kant's hope, common reason seems to deploy most of its time and energy in the service of disarming and incapacitating the demands and pressures of the allegedly categorical imperative. According to the precepts of reason, the most reasonable, most worthy of attention and most commendable principles of action are those of pre-empting or abolishing the symmetry between the actors and the objects of their actions; or at least those stratagems that, once deployed, reduce to a minimum the chances of reciprocation. Whatever 'stands to reason' all too often flatly refuses to 'stand to demands of morality'. At any rate, it loses none of its reason-ableness when it fails a moral test.

Reason is a service station of power. It is, first and foremost, a factory of might (*Macht, pouvoir*), defined as the subject's capacity to reach objectives despite the resistance – whether of inert matter or of subjects pursuing different aims. 'To be mighty' means, in other words, the ability to overcome the inertia of a recalcitrant object of action or to ignore the ambitions of other *dramatis personae* (to wit, to enjoy the sole subjectivity and the sole effec-tive intentionality in the multi-actor drama, and so reduce the other subjects to the status of the objects of action or its neutral backdrop). By its very nature, might and power are asymmetrical (one is tempted to say: just as nature stands no void, power stands no symmetry). Power does not unify and does not level up (or down) differences; power divides and opposes. Power is a sworn enemy and suppressor of symmetry, reciprocity and mutuality. Power's might consists in its potency to manipulate probabilities and differentiate possibilities as well as potentialities and chances: all through sealing up the resulting divisions and immunizing inequalities of distribution against dissent and appeals from those at the receiving end of the operation.

In a nutshell, power and the might to act, the production and the servicing of which are the calling of reason, equal an explicit rejection or ignoring in practice of the presumption which renders Kant's imperative categorical. As vividly and poignantly expressed by Friedrich Nietzsche:

> What is good? All that enhances the feeling of power . . . What is bad? All that proceeds from weakness . . . The weak and the botched shall perish: first principle of our humanity. And they

ought even be helped to perish. What is more harmful than any
vice? – Practical sympathy with all the botched and weak . . .[4]

'I know joy in destruction', Nietzsche admitted, proudly. 'I am
therewith *destroyer par excellence.*'[5] Several generations of other
'destroyers par excellence', armed with weapons adequate to
making the words flesh (and more to the point, to make the
words *kill* the flesh), who worked hard to make Nietzsche's vision
reality, could draw inspiration there – and many among them did.
They would find absolution for their intention in Nietzsche's
exhortation to help the weak and the botched to perish. As
Zarathustra, Nietzsche's authorized spokesman and plenipoten-
tiary, puts it: 'My greatest danger always lay in indulgence and
sufferance; and all humankind wants to be indulged and suffered.'[6] The verdicts of Nature can be tinkered with only at the
tinkerers' peril and ruin. To avoid ruin, humans must be freed:
the high and mighty from pity, compassion, (unjustly) guilty
conscience and (uncalled for) *scruples* – and the vulgar and lowly
from *hope*.

Efforts to crack one mystery that perhaps more than any other
keeps ethical philosophers awake at night, namely the mystery
of *unde malum* (whence evil?), and more specifically and yet more
urgently of 'how good people turn evil'[7] (or, more to the point,
the secret of the mysterious transmogrification of caring family
people, and friendly and benevolent neighbours, into monsters),
were triggered and given a first powerful push by the rising
tide of twentieth-century totalitarianism, set in feverish motion
by the Holocaust revelations, and accelerated still further by
growing evidence of an ever more noticeable likeness between the
post-Holocaust world and a minefield, of which one knows that
an explosion must occur sooner or later, yet no one knows when
and where.

From the start, the efforts to crack the aforementioned mystery
have followed three different tracks; in all probability, they will
continue to follow all three of them for a long time to come, as
none of the three trajectories seems to possess a final station where
the explorers can rest satisfied they have reached the intended
destination of their journey. The purpose of their exploration is,
after all, to catch in the net of reason the kinds of phenomena

described by Günther Anders as 'over-liminal' (*überschwellige*): phenomena that cannot be grasped and intellectually assimilated because they outgrow any sensual or conceptual nets, thereby sharing the fate of their apparent opposite, 'subliminal' (*unterschwellige*) phenomena – tiny and fast moving enough to escape even the densest of nets, and to vanish before they can be caught and sent over to reason for intelligent recycling.

The first track (most recently seeming to be taken by Jonathan Littell in his book *The Kindly Ones*,[8] with only a few, less than crucial, qualifications) leads to a delving into and fathoming of *psychical* peculiarities (or psychical sediments of biographical peculiarities) discovered or hypothesized among *individuals* who are known to have committed cruel acts or who have been caught red-handed, these are therefore assumed to outdo average individuals in their inclination and eagerness to commit atrocities when they are tempted or commanded to do so. That track was laid even before the monstrous human deeds of the post-Holocaust era revealed the full awesomeness of the potential scale of the problem. It was started by Theodore Adorno's highly influential and memorable 'authoritarian personality' study, promoting the idea of, so to speak, the self-selection of the evildoers – and suggesting that the self-selection in question was determined by natural rather than nurtured predispositions of individual character.

Another, perhaps the widest and most massively trodden track, was laid along the line of behavioural *conditioning* and led to an investigation of the types of social positionings or situations that might prompt individuals – 'normal' under 'ordinary' or the most common circumstances – to join in the perpetration of evil deeds; or, to express it another way, conditions awakening evil predispositions that under different conditions would have remained fast asleep. For scholars following this track, it was society of a certain type, not certain individual features, that belonged on the defendant's bench. Siegfried Kracauer, for instance, or Hans Speier, sought in the unstoppably multiplying ranks of the *Angestellte* (office workers) the source of the foul moral atmosphere that favoured recruitment to the army of evil. That malodorous, indeed morally poisonous atmosphere was shortly afterwards ascribed by Hannah Arendt to the 'proto-totalitarian' predispositions of the bourgeois, or to the philistinism and vulgarity of classes forcibly reforged into masses (following the principle of 'Erst kommt das Fressen, dann kommt die Moral', as Bertolt Brecht succinctly put it).[9]

Hannah Arendt, arguably the most prominent spokesperson for this way of thinking, sharply and uncompromisingly opposing the reduction of social phenomena to the individual psyche, observed that the true genius among the Nazi seducers was Himmler, who – neither descending from bohemianism as Goebbels did, nor being a sexual pervert like Julius Streicher, an adventurer like Goering, a fanatic like Hitler or a madman like Alfred Rosenberg – 'organized the masses into a system of total domination', thanks to his (correct!) assumption that in their decisive majority men are not vampires or sadists, but job-holders and family providers.[10] Where that observation ultimately led her, we can learn from her book *Eichmann in Jerusalem*. The most widely quoted of Arendt's conclusions was her succinct verdict of the banality of evil. What Arendt meant when she pronounced that verdict was that monstrosities do not need monsters, outrages do not need outrageous characters, and that the trouble with Eichmann lay precisely in the fact that, according to the assessments of supreme luminaries of psychology and psychiatry, he (alongside so many of his companions in crime) was not a monster or a sadist, but outrageously, terribly, frighteningly 'normal'. Littell would at least partly follow that conclusion of Arendt's in his insistence that Eichmann was anything but a 'faceless, soulless robot'. Among the most recent studies following that line, *The Lucifer Effect* by Philip Zimbardo, published in 2007, is a blood-curdling and nerve-racking study of a bunch of good, ordinary, likeable and popular American lads and lasses who turned into monsters once they had been transported to a sort of 'nowhere place', to the faraway country of Iraq, and put in charge of prisoners charged with ill intentions and suspected of belonging to an inferior brand of human being, or possibly being somewhat less than human.

How safe and comfortable, cosy and friendly the world would feel if it were monsters and monsters alone who perpetrated monstrous deeds. Against monsters we are fairly well protected, and so we can rest assured that we are insured against the evil deeds that monsters are capable of and threaten to perpetrate. We have psychologists to spot psychopaths and sociopaths, we have sociologists to tell us where they are likely to propagate and congregate, we have judges to condemn them to confinement and isolation, and police or psychiatrists to make sure they stay there. Alas, the good, ordinary, likeable American lads and lasses were neither monsters nor perverts. Had they not been assigned to lord over the inmates of Abu Ghraib, we would *never* have known (surmised, guessed, imagined, fantasized) the horrifying things they were capable of contriving. It wouldn't occur to any of us that the smiling girl at the counter might, once on overseas assignment, excel at devising ever more clever and fanciful, as well as wicked and perverse tricks to harass, molest, torture and humiliate her wards. In her and her companions' hometowns, their neighbours refuse to believe to this very day that those charming lads and lasses they have known since their childhoods are the same folk as the monsters in the snapshots of the Abu Ghraib torture chambers. But they are.

In the conclusion of his psychological study of Chip Frederick, the suspected leader and guide of the torturers' pack, Philip Zimbardo had to say that there was absolutely nothing in his record that he was able to uncover that would have predicted that Chip Frederick would engage in any form of abusive, sadistic behaviour. On the contrary, there was much in his record to suggest that had he not been forced to work and live in such an abnormal situation, he might have been the military's all-American poster soldier on its recruitment ads.

Indeed, Chip Frederick would have passed with flying colours any imaginable psychological test, as well as the most thorough scrutiny of the record of behaviour routinely applied in selecting candidates for the most responsible and morally sensitive services, such as those of the official, uniformed guardians of law and order. In the case of Chip Frederick and his closest and most notorious companion, Lynndie England, you might still insist (even if counterfactually) that they had acted on command and had been forced to engage in atrocities they detested and abhorred – meek sheep rather than predatory wolves. The sole charge against them you might then approve would be that of cowardice or exaggerated respect for their superiors; at the utmost, the charge of having too easily, without as much as a murmur of protest, abandoned the moral principles which guided them in their 'ordinary' life at home. But what about those at the top of bureaucratic ladder?

Those who gave commands, forced obedience and punished the disobedient? Those people, surely, must have been monsters?

The inquiry into the Abu Ghraib outrage never reached the top echelons of the American military command; for the top, command-issuing people to be brought to account and tried for war crimes, they would first need to find themselves on the defeated side in the war they waged – which they did not. But Adolf Eichmann, presiding over the tools and procedures of the 'final solution' of the 'Jewish problem' and giving orders to their operators, was on the side of the defeated, had been captured by victors and brought to their courts. There was occasion, therefore, to submit the 'monster hypothesis' to a most careful, indeed meticulous scrutiny – and by the most distinguished members of the psychological and psychiatric professions. The final conclusion drawn from that most thorough and reliable research was anything but ambiguous. Here it is, as conveyed by Hannah Arendt:

> Half a dozen psychiatrists had certified him as 'normal' – 'More normal, at any rate, than I am after examining him', one of them was said to have exclaimed, while another had found that his whole psychological outlook, his attitude towards wife and children, mother and father, brothers, sisters and friends was 'not only normal but most desirable'. . . . The trouble with Eichmann was precisely that so many were like him, and that the many were neither perverted nor sadistic, that they were, and still are, terribly and terrifyingly normal. From the viewpoint of our legal institutions and our moral standards of judgment, this normality was much more terrifying than all the atrocities put together . . .[11]

It must indeed have been the most terrifying of findings: if it is not ogres but normal people (I am tempted to add 'guys like you and me') who commit atrocities and are capable of acting in a perverted and sadistic way, then all the sieves we've invented and put in place to strain out the carriers of inhumanity from the rest of the human species are either botched in execution or misconceived from the start – and most certainly ineffective. And so we are, to cut a long story short, *un*protected (one is tempted to add 'defenceless against our shared morbid capacity'). Employing their ingenuity to the utmost and trying as hard as they could to 'civilize' human manners and the patterns of human togetherness, our ancestors, and also those of us who have followed their line of thought and action, are, so to speak, barking up a wrong tree . . .

Reading *The Kindly Ones* attentively, one can unpack a covert critique of the common interpretation, endorsed by Arendt herself, of the 'banality of evil' thesis: namely, the supposition that the evildoer Eichmann was an 'unthinking man'. From Littell's portrayal, Eichmann emerges as anything but an unthinking follower of orders or a slave to his own base passions. 'He was certainly not an *enemy of mankind* described in Nuremberg,' 'nor was he an incarnation of *banal evil*', he was on the contrary 'a very talented bureaucrat, extremely competent at his functions, with a certain stature and a considerable sense of personal initiative'.[12] As a manager, Eichmann would most certainly be the pride of any reputable European firm (one could add, including companies with Jewish owners or top executives). Littell's narrator, Dr Aue, insists that in the many personal encounters he had with Eichmann he never noticed any trace of a personal prejudice against, let alone a passionate hatred, of the Jews, whom he saw as no more, though no less either, than objects which his office demanded to be duly processed. Whether at home or in his job, Eichmann was consistently the same person, the kind of person he was, for instance, when he performed two Brahms quartets with his SS mates: 'Eichmann played calmly, methodically, his eyes riveted to the score; he didn't make any mistakes.'[13]

If Eichmann was 'normal', then no one is a priori exempt from suspicion – none of our dazzlingly normal friends and acquaintances; and neither are we. Chip Fredericks and Adolf Eichmanns walk our streets in full view, queue like us at the checkouts of the same shops, fill cinemas and football grandstands, travel on trains and city buses or get stuck next to us in traffic jams. They might live next door, or even sit at our dining table. All of them, given propitious circumstances, might do what Chip Frederick or Adolf Eichmann did. And what about me?! Since so many people can potentially commit acts of humanity, I might easily by chance, by a mere caprice of fate, become one of their victims. *They* can do it – I already know that. But isn't it also the case that equally easily *I myself* might become one of 'them': just another 'ordinary human' who can do to other humans what they have done . . .

John M. Steiner used the metaphor of a 'sleeper',[14] drawn from the terminology of spy networks, to denote an as yet undisclosed personal inclination to commit acts of violence, or a person's vulnerability to the temptation to join in such acts – an odious potential that may hypothetically be present in particular individuals while long remaining invisible; an inclination that can (is bound to?) surface, or a vulnerability that may be revealed, only under some particularly propitious conditions, presumably once the forces that hitherto repressed it and kept it under cover are abruptly weakened or removed. Ervin Staub moved one (gigantic) step further, deleting both references to 'particularity' in Steiner's proposition and hypothesizing the presence of malevolent 'sleepers' in most, perhaps all human beings: 'Evil . . . committed by ordinary people is the norm, not an exception.' Is he right? We don't know and never will know, at least never know for sure, because there is no way to prove or disprove that guess empirically. Possibilities are not unlike chickens: they can be reliably and definitely counted only once they are hatched.

What do we know for sure? The ease 'with which sadistic behaviour could be elicited in individuals who were not "sadistic types"' was discovered by Zimbardo in his earlier experiments conducted at Stanford University with students randomly selected to play the role of 'prison guards' towards fellow students, also randomly cast in the role of prisoners.[15] Stanley Milgram, in his Yale experiments with people, again randomly chosen, who were asked to inflict on other people a series of what they were made to believe were painful electric shocks of escalating magnitude found that 'obedience to authority', any authority, regardless of the nature of the commands given by that authority, is a 'deeply ingrained behaviour tendency' even if the subjects find the actions they are told to perform repugnant and revolting.[16] If you add to that factor such well-nigh universal sediments of socialization as the attributes of loyalty, sense of duty and discipline, 'men are led to kill with little difficulty'. It is easy, in other words, to prod, push, seduce and entice non-evil people to commit evil things.

Christopher R. Browning investigated the twisted yet invariably gory path of men belonging to the German Reserve Police Battalion 101, assigned to the police from among conscripts unfit for frontline duty, and eventually delegated to participate in the mass murder of Jews in Poland.[17] Those people, who had never been known to commit violent, let alone murderous acts up till then, and gave no grounds for suspicion that they were capable of committing them, were ready (not 100 per cent of them, but a considerable majority) to comply with the command to murder: to shoot, point blank, men and women, old people and children, who were unarmed and obviously innocent since they had not been charged with any crime, none of whom nurturing the slightest intention to harm them or their comrades-in-arms. What Browning found, however (and published under the tell-all title of *Ordinary Men*), was that only about 10 to 20 per cent of the conscripted policemen proved to be 'refusers and evaders', who asked to be excused from carrying out the orders, that there was also 'a nucleus of increasingly enthusiastic killers who volunteered for the firing squads and "Jew hunts"', but that by far the largest group of conscript policemen placidly performed the role of murderers and ghetto clearers when it was assigned to them, though without seeking opportunities to kill on their own initiative. The most striking aspect of that finding was in my view the amazing similarity of Browning's statistical distribution of zealots, abstainers and impassioned 'neither–nors' to that of the reactions of the subjects of Zimbardo's and Milgram's experiments to the authoritatively endorsed commands. In all three cases, some people ordered to commit cruelty were only too eager to leap to the occasion and give vent to their evil drives; some – roughly the same number – refused to do evil whatever the circumstances and whatever the consequences of their abstention; whereas an extensive 'middle ground' was filled by people who were indifferent, lukewarm and not particularly engaged or strongly committed to one or the other end of the attitudinal spectrum, avoiding taking any stand, whether for morality or against it, and preferring instead to follow the line of least resistance and do whatever prudence dictated, and unconcern allowed.

In other words, in all three cases (as well as in innumerable others in the extensive set of studies of which these three investigations have been acclaimed as the most spectacular and illuminating examples), the distribution of probabilities that the command to do evil will be obeyed or resisted has followed the standard known in statistics as the Gaussian curve (sometimes called the Gaussian bell, Gaussian distribution, or Gaussian function), believed to be the graph of the most common and prototypical, to wit 'normal', distribution of probabilities. We read in Wikipedia that what the notion of the Gaussian curve refers to is the tendency of results to 'cluster around a mean or average'. 'The graph of the associated probability density function is bell-shaped, with a peak at the mean.' We also read that 'by the central limit theorem, any variable that is the sum of a large number of independent factors is likely to be normally distributed'.

As the probabilities of various behavioural responses by people exposed to the pressure to do evil show a clear tendency to take the form of a Gaussian curve, we can risk the supposition that, in their case as well, the results were compounded by the mutual interference of a large number of independent factors: commands descending from on high, instinctual or deeply entrenched respect for or fear of authority, loyalty reinforced by considerations of duty and drilled discipline – these were some of them, but not necessarily the only ones.

The possible silver lining to this uniformly dark cloud is that it seems plausible (just plausible . . .) that under conditions of liquid modernity, marked by a loosening or dissipation of bureaucratic hierarchies of authority, as well as by the multiplication of sites from which competitive recommendations are voiced (the two factors responsible for the rising incoherence and diminishing audibility of those voices), other, more individual, idiosyncratic and personal factors, for instance personal character, may play an increasingly important role in the choice of responses. The humanity of humans might gain if they did.

And yet our shared experience thus far offers few, if any, reasons to be optimistic. As W. G. Sebald suggests (in his 1999 *Luftkrieg und Literatur*, translated by Anthea Bell as *On the Natural History of Destruction*), 'we are unable to learn from the misfortunes we bring on ourselves' and 'we are incorrigible and will continue along the beaten tracks that bear some slight relation to the old road network'.[18] Bent as we all are, by nature or training, on seeking and finding the shortest way to the aims we pursue and believe to be worth pursuing, 'misfortunes' (and particularly misfortunes suffered by others) do not seem an excessively high price to pay for shortening the route, cutting costs and magnifying the effects.

Sebald quotes, after Alexander Kluge's *Unheimlichkeit der Zeit*, an interview conducted by a German journalist, Kunzert, with the US Eighth Army Air Force Brigadier Frederick L. Anderson.

Pressed by Kunzert to explain whether there was a way to prevent or avoid the destruction of Halberstadt, his home town, by American carpet bombing, Anderson responded that the bombs were, after all, 'expensive items'. 'In practice, they couldn't have been dropped over mountains or open country after so much labour had gone into making them at home.'[19] Anderson, uncommonly frank, hit the nail on the head; it was not the need to do something about Halberstadt that decided the use of the bombs, but the need to do something with the bombs that decided the fate of Halberstadt. Halberstadt was just a 'collateral casualty' (to update the language of the military) of the success of the bomb factories. As Sebald explains, 'once the matériel was manufactured, simply letting the aircraft and their valuable freight stand idle on the airfields of eastern England ran counter to any healthy economic instinct'.[20]

That 'economic instinct' might perhaps have had the first, but most certainly did have the last word in the debate about the propriety and usefulness of the strategy of Sir Arthur ('Bomber') Harris: the destruction of German cities went into full and unstoppable swing well after the spring of 1944, when it had already dawned on policy makers and the givers of military orders that – contrary to the officially proclaimed objective of the air campaign and its protracted, determined, lavish and zealous execution, pulling no punches, – 'the morale of the German population was obviously unbroken, while industrial production was impaired only marginally at best, and the end of the war had not come a day closer'. By the time of that discovery, and disclosure, 'the matériel' in question had already been manufactured and was filling the warehouses to capacity; letting it lie idle would indeed 'counter any healthy economic instinct', or, to put it simply, would make no 'economic sense' (according to an estimate by A. J. P. Taylor, quoted by Max Hastings in his 1979 study *Bomber Command*, p. 349, the servicing of the bombing campaign after all engaged and 'swallowed up' one-third of total British production servicing the war).

We have so far sketched and compared two tracks along which the search for an answer to the *unde malum* has proceeded in recent times. There is, however, a third track, too, which due to the universality and extemporality of the factors it invokes and deploys in the pursuit of understanding deserves to be called *anthropological*. This is a perspective that with the passage of time seems to rise in importance and promise, just as the other two sketched above near the exhaustion of their cognitive potential. We could intuit the direction of that third track in Sebald's study. It had already been laid out before, however, in Günther Anders' seminal study, overlooked or neglected for a few decades, of the phenomenon of the 'Nagasaki syndrome', charged by Anders with the fully and truly apocalyptic potential of 'globocide'.[21] The 'Nagasaki syndrome', Anders suggested, means that 'what has been done once can be repeated over again, with ever weaker reservations'; with each successive case, more and more 'matter-of-factly, casually, with little deliberation or motive'. 'The repetition of outrage is not just possible, but probable – as the chance to win the battle to prevent it gets smaller, while that of losing it rises.'

The decision to drop atomic bombs on Hiroshima on 6 August 1945, and three days later on Nagasaki, was officially explained, ex post facto, by the need to bring forward the capitulation of Japan in order to save the countless American lives which most certainly would have been lost if the American army had had to invade the Japanese archipelago. The jury of history is still in session, but the official version of the motive, justifying the meanness and villainy of the means by reference to the grandiosity and nobility of the goals, has been recently cast into doubt by American historians examining newly declassified information about the circumstances in which the decision was considered, taken and implemented, allowing the official version to be questioned not only on moral, but also on factual grounds. As the critics of the official version aver, the rulers of Japan were ready to capitulate a month or so before the first atom bomb was dropped – and just two steps would have caused them to lay down arms: Truman's consent to the Soviet Army joining the war with Japan, and the commitments of the allies to keep the Emperor on his throne after Japan's surrender.

Truman, however, procrastinated. He waited for the results of the test which was set to be conducted in Alamogordo in New Mexico, where final touches were about to be put on the performance of the first atomic bombs. The news of the results did arrive, in Potsdam on 17 July: the test was not just successful – the impact of the explosion eclipsed the boldest of expectations . . . Resenting the idea of consigning an exorbitantly expensive technology to waste, Truman started playing for time. The genuine stake of his procrastination could easily be deduced from the triumphant presidential address published in the *New York Times* on the day following the destruction of a hundred thousand lives in Hiroshima: 'We made the most audacious scientific bet in history, a bet of 2 billion dollars – and won.' One just couldn't waste 2 billion dollars, could one? If the original objective is reached before the product has had a chance to be used, one has to promptly find another aim that will preserve or restore 'economic sense' to the expenditure . . .

On 16 March 1945, when Nazi Germany was already on its knees and the speedy end of the war was no longer in doubt, Arthur 'Bomber' Harris sent out 225 Lancaster bombers and eleven Mosquito fighter planes with orders to discharge 289 tons of explosives and 573 tons of incendiary substances on Würzburg, a middle-sized town with 107,000 residents, rich in history and art treasures, and poor in industry. Between 9.20 and 9.37 p.m. about 5,000 inhabitants (of whom 66 per cent were women and 14 per cent children) were killed, while 21,000 dwelling houses were set on fire: only 6,000 residents still found a roof over their heads once the planes had left. Hermann Knell, who calculated the figures above after scrupulous scrutiny of the archives,[22] asks why a town devoid of any kind of strategic significance (an opinion confirmed, even if in a roundabout way, by the omission of any mention of that town's name in the official history of the Royal Air Force, which meticulously lists all its accomplishments, even the most minute) was selected for destruction. Having examined all conceivable alternative causes, and disqualified them one by one, Knell was left with the sole sensible answer to his question: that Arthur Harris and Carl Spaatz (the commander of the US Air Force in Great Britain and Italy) found themselves short of targets at the beginning of 1945:

> The bombing progressed as planned without consideration of the changed military situation. The destruction of German cities continued until the end of April. Seemingly once the military

machine was moving it could not be stopped. It had a life of its own. There was now all the equipment and soldiers on hand. It must have been that aspect that made Harris decide to have Würzburg attacked . . .

But why Würzburg of all places? Purely for reasons of convenience. As previous reconnaissance sorties had shown, 'the city could easily be located with the electronic aids available at the time'. And the city was sufficiently distant from the advancing allied troops to reduce the threat of another case of 'friendly fire' (i.e., dropping bombs on one's own troops). In other words, the town was 'an easy and riskless target'. This was Würzburg's inadvertent and unwitting fault, a kind of fault for which no 'target' would ever be pardoned once 'the military machine was moving' . . .

In *La Violence nazie: une généalogie européenne* Enzo Traverso puts forward a concept of the 'barbaric potential' of modern civilization.[23] In his study dedicated to Nazi violence he comes to the conclusion that the Nazi-style atrocities were unique solely in the sense of synthesizing a large number of the means of enslavement and annihilation already tested, though separately, in the history of Western civilization.

> The bombs dropped on Hiroshima and Nagasaki prove that anti-Enlightenment sentiments are not necessary conditions of technological massacre. The two atomic bombs, like the Nazi camps, were elements of the 'civilizing process', manifestations of one of its potentials, one of its faces and one of its possible ramifications.

Traverso finishes his exploration with a warning that there are no grounds whatsoever for excluding the possibility of other syntheses in the future – ones no less murderous than those of the Nazis. The liberal, civilized Europe of the twentieth century proved to be, after all, a laboratory of violence. Myself, I'd add that there are no signs of that laboratory having been shut or of operation ceasing at the dawn of the twenty-first century.

Günther Anders asks: are we, in this age of machines, the last relics of the past who have not as yet managed to clean off the toxic sediments of past atrocities?[24] And he answers: the outrages under discussion were committed *then* not because they were *still* feasible (or had *so far* failed to be eradicated), but on the contrary, they were *already* perpetrated then because then they had *already* become feasible and plausible . . .

Let me sum up: there must have been a 'first moment' when the technologically assisted atrocities that had been inconceivable until then became feasible. Those atrocities must have had their moment of beginning, their starting point – but it does not follow that they must have an end as well. It does not follow that they entered human cohabitation only for a brief visit, and even less that they brought with them or set in motion mechanisms that were bound sooner or later to cause their departure. It is rather the other way round: once a contraption allowing the separation of technological capacity from moral imagination is put in place, it becomes self-propelling, self-reinforcing and self-reinvigorating. The human capacity to adjust, habituate, become accustomed, to start today from the point reached the evening before, and all in all to recycle the inconceivability of yesterday into today's fact of the matter will see to that.

Atrocities, in other words, do not self-condemn and self-destruct. They, on the contrary, self-reproduce: what was once an unexpectedly horrifying turn of fate and a shock (an awesome discovery, a gruesome revelation) degenerates into a routine conditioned reflex. Hiroshima was a shock with deafeningly loud and seemingly inextinguishable echoes. Three days later, Nagasaki was hardly a shock, evoking few if any echoes. Joseph Roth has pointed to one of the mechanisms of that desensitizing habituation:

> When a catastrophe occurs, people at hand are shocked into helpfulness. Certainly, acute catastrophes have that effect. It seems that people expect catastrophes to be brief. But chronic catastrophes are so unpalatable to neighbours that they gradually become indifferent to them and their victims, if not downright impatient . . . Once the emergency becomes protracted, helping hands return to pockets, the fires of compassion cool down.[25]

In other words, a protracted catastrophe blazes the trail of its own continuation by consigning the initial shock and outrage to oblivion and thus emaciates and enfeebles human solidarity with its victims, so sapping the possibility of joining forces for the sake of staving off future victimization . . .

But how and why did the said atrocities come to be in the first place? For explorers of the sources of evil, it is Anders, it seems, who sketches yet another approach, best called *metaphysical*. Its antecedents can be detected in Heidegger's concept of *techne*, though curiously that acclaimed metaphysician of being-in-time set techne beyond historical time, in the metaphysics of *Sein* – being – *as such*, thereby presenting techne as a history-immune, intractable and unchangeable attribute of all and any being. Anders, on the other hand, is intensely aware of the intimate interdependence of techne and history and the sensitivity of techne to the historical transmutations of forms of life. Anders, it can be seen, focused on a metaphysics of evil made to the measure of our times, a specific evil, uniquely endemic to our own present and still continuing form of human cohabitation: a form defined and set apart from other forms by a techne (a product, in the last account, of the human power of imagination) racing far *beyond human imagining powers* and in its turn overpowering, enslaving and disabling the very human capacity that brought it into being. A prototype of the convoluted, meandering story of Andersian 'techne' needs to be sought, perhaps, in the ancient saga of the sorcerer's wayward apprentice, Hegel's and Marx's physiology of alienation, and closer to our times in Georg Simmel's idea of the 'tragedy of culture' – of the products of the human spirit rising to a volume transcending and leaving far behind the human power of absorption, comprehension, assimilation and mastery.

According to Anders, the human power to produce (*herstellen*: having things done, plans implemented) has been emancipated in recent decades from the constraints imposed by the much less expandable power of humans to imagine, represent and render intelligible (*vorstellen*). It is in that relatively new phenomenon, the hiatus (*Diskrepanz*) separating the human powers of creation and imagination, that the contemporary variety of evil sets its roots. The moral calamity of our time 'does not grow from our sensuality or perfidy, dishonesty or licentiousness, nor even from exploitation – but from a deficit of imagination'; whereas imagination, as Anders untiringly insists, grasps more of the 'truth' (*nimmt mehr 'wahr'*), than our machine-driven empirical perception (*Wahrnehmung*) is capable of.[26] I would add: imagination also grasps infinitely more of the *moral* truth, in encountering which our empirical perception is especially blindfolded.

The reality grasped by perception orphaned by imagination, and beyond which it is unable to reach, is always-already-made, technologically prefabricated and operated; there is no room in it for those thousands or millions cast at its receiving end and sentenced to destruction by atomic bombs, napalm or poisonous gas. That reality consists of keyboards and pushbuttons. And, as Anders points out, 'one doesn't gnash one's teeth when pressing a button ... A key is a key.'[27] Whether the pressing of the key starts a kitchen contraption making ice-cream, feeds current into an electricity network or lets loose the Horsemen of the Apocalypse makes no difference. 'The gesture that will initiate the Apocalypse will not differ from any of the other gestures – and it will be performed, like all the other identical gestures, by an operator similarly guided and bored by routine.' 'If something symbolizes the satanic nature of our situation, it is precisely that innocence of the gesture;'[28] the negligibility of the effort and thought needed to set off a cataclysm – any cataclysm, including globocide. *We are technologically all-powerful because of, and thanks to, the powerlessness of our imagination.*

Powerless as we are, we are omnipotent, since we are capable of bringing into being forces able in their turn to cause effects which we wouldn't be able to produce with our 'natural equipment' – our own hands and muscles. But having become all-powerful in that way, watching and admiring the might and efficiency and the shattering effects of entities we have ourselves designed and conjured up, we discover our own powerlessness ... That discovery comes together with another: that of the *pride* of inventing and setting in motion magnificent machines able to perform Herculean deeds which we would be otherwise incapable of performing. By the same token, we feel *challenged*, however, by the standards of perfection we've set for the machines brought into being by us, but which we ourselves can't match. And so, finally, we discover *shame*: the ignominy of our own inferiority, and thus the humiliation which overwhelms us when we face up to our own impotence.

Those three discoveries combine, as Anders suggests, into the 'Promethean complex'. Anders has names for the objects of each discovery: Promethean pride, Promethean challenge, and Promethean shame.[29] The latter is the sense of one's own inborn inferiority and imperfection, both blatant once they are juxtaposed with the perfection, nay omnipotence, of made-up things; the outcome of the indignity brought upon us in the last account by our failure to self-reify, to become *like* the machines: indomitable, irresistible, unstoppable, unsubmissive and indeed ungovernable, as the machines are 'at their best'. To mitigate that infamy, we need to demonstrate our own ability to accomplish, by our own natural means and bodily effort and without the help of the machines, things which the machines so easily, matter-of-factly perform: by turning themselves, in other words, into means for the means, tools for the tools . . . when they had watched from their low-flying war machines, avidly and at close quarters, the ravages perpetrated by the tools of murder and devastation sprinkled over the village of My Lai, Lieutenant Calley's soldiers could not resist the challenge or temptation to perform personally, with their bare hands, what their weapons achieved mechanically: the temptation to catch up with the tools of destruction and to overtake them in the chase for perfection – if only for a moment and only here and now, in this village.[30] The sight of inanimate objects harnessed to the gory job widened the soldiers' *horizons*, uncovered unthought-of *possibilities*, stimulated the *imagination* – but these were horizons already drawn by machines, possibilities opened up by mechanical conduct, and imagination industrially prefabricated.

In his second open letter to Klaus Eichmann,[31] Anders writes of the relation between the criminal Nazi state and the post-Nazi, contemporary, world regime: 'The affinity between the technical-totalitarian empire which threatens us and the monstrous Nazi empire is evident.' But he hastens to explain right away that he intends the above statement as a provocation, aimed against the widespread (because comforting) opinion that the Third Reich was a unique phenomenon, an aberration untypical of our times and particularly in our Western world; an opinion which owes its popularity to its treacherous potency in exonerating and legitimizing a turning away of one's eyes from one's own gruesome, terrifying potential. Personally, I deeply regret that I was not aware of these conclusions of Anders, when I was working on my *Modernity and the Holocaust*.

In response to a journalist's suggestion that he belongs in the ranks of 'panicmongers', Anders replied that he considers the title of 'panicmonger' to be a distinction and wears it with pride – adding that 'in our days, the most important moral task is to make people aware that they need to be alarmed – and that the fears that haunt them have valid reasons'.[32]

10

Wir arme Leut' . . .

Wir arme Leut' (Wretches like us) is what Wozzeck says in the first act of Alban Berg's opera when he sings in his own defence against the charges of indecency and lack of chastity that the Captain and the Doctor – well-educated, well-off and well-respected persons – heap upon him. Wozzeck has failed to live up to the standards of propriety and seemliness they have set, believe themselves to be following and demand all others to obey and respect; at least that is what the Captain and the Doctor said. They scoffed at Wozzeck, derided and reviled him for being so jarringly *unlike them*. They blamed his baseness, coarseness and vulgarity for that abominable and unforgivable sin. *Wir arme Leut'*, Wozzeck replies, could not live like you do, however hard we tried . . . In the game of virtue and vice, the rules have been set by you and others *like* you, and so you find them easy to follow; but you would find it hard to follow them if you were as poor as *wir, die arme Leute* are. Please note that Wozzeck says *Wir*: not *ich* ('we' not 'I')! In other words, 'What you blame me for', he might have explained, 'is not my *personal* fault. It is not I alone who fall beneath the standards you set. There are many failures just like me. Censuring me, you censure all those many – all of us.'

But who are those 'us' whom Wozzeck calls to bear him witness?

To be poor is to be lonely . . .

Wozzeck does not refer to a class, a race, an ethnicity, a faith, a nation . . . to any of those commonly brandished bodies that tacitly assume and vociferously aver themselves to be communities: groups that think of themselves as (for better or worse) united – by their shared past, present condition and future fate, by their few joys and many sorrows, few strokes of luck and many misfortunes. Groups demanding loyalty from their members, being born of that loyalty, and resurrected daily by their members' continuing dedication. Groups that expect all their members to share responsibility for each other's well-being, and fight together against each other's ill-being. Groups that know who is a member ('one of *us*'), and who is not (being therefore 'one of *them*'), that draw a boundary between 'us' and 'them', and try hard to control the border traffic. In Wozzeck's invocation to 'wir arme Leut', such a community is present only as a ghost: present through its (regrettable, bewailed) *absence*.

But please note that what matters most in Georg Büchner's drama are not Wozzeck's few frugal and slight speeches, but his rarely broken, ample, copious, and (sic!) eloquent silences. There is no invocation to communities in Wozzeck's speeches. It is as if Wozzeck obeyed Ludwig Wittgenstein's injunction: 'About what one can't speak of, one must keep silent'. About communities Wozzeck kept silent, since there were no, and are no, communities of which he could speak. And so, in his desperate search for apology and self-defence, he invoked *arme Leut'*. *Arme Leut'* do not form a community. Rather than uniting them, their misery sets them apart and divides them. Poor people bear their pains individually, as they stand individually accused for their (individually caused and individually suffered) defeats and misery. Each one of them has landed in the category of *arme Leut'* due to her or his own, individual faults, and each one licks his or her individual wounds alone.

Arme Leute may envy or fear each other; sometimes they may pity, or even (though not too often) like one another. None of them, however, would ever *respect* another creature 'like him' (or her). If those other people are indeed 'like' I am myself, they must be unworthy of respect and deserve contempt and derision just as I do! *Arme Leute* have good reason to refuse respect and not to expect to be respected in their turn: their *Armut, Ärmlichkeit, Armseligkeit* (poverty, humbleness, wretchedness), signalling material deprivation, undoubtedly a miserable and painful condition, are also indelible traces, and vivid evidence, of indignity and social disrespect. They testify that those in authority, people who have the power to allow or to refuse rights, have refused to grant them the rights due to other, 'normal' humans. And so they testify, by proxy, to the humiliation and self-contempt that inevitably follow social endorsement of personal unworthiness and ignominy. If the only name Wozzeck could use when referring to 'others like me' was *arme Leute*, then what he obliquely, knowingly or not, betrayed was his exclusion from the family of 'normal' humans. And his banishment from the communities he knew and knew of, without an invitation to join another, and no prospect of being allowed admission to any other.

. . . Among the lonely . . .

If Andreas Kriegenburg, the director of the 2008 Bavarian State Opera production, were to rewrite the words of Wozzeck's song in the idiom of its viewers and listeners, he could perhaps replace *Wir arme Leute* with *Wir, die Unterklasse*. The 'Unterklasse' ('underclass') is not a community but a category. The sole attribute shared by every human assigned to that category is the stigma of estrangement, of having been excluded. It is the stigma of a total exclusion, from all the sites and situations where all other human identities and titles to recognition are made, negotiated, remade or unmade. Being totally excluded by being relegated to the 'underclass' means being stripped of all socially produced and socially accepted trappings and marks that elevate mere biological life to the rank of a social being, and herds into communities. The underclass is not merely an absence of community; it is the sheer *impossibility of community*. Ultimately, this also means the impossibility of humanity – because it is only through a network of communities, holding the rights to accord and to endorse a socially legible and respected identity, that humanity may be entered. As Aristotle pointed out almost two and a half millennia ago, one cannot be human – or, being human, cannot survive – outside a 'polis'; only angels and beasts can exist outside a polis, he added.

Socrates must have been of the same opinion, since, being neither angel nor beast, he preferred a bowl of hemlock to banishment from Athens.

The underclass is, however, also a liminal category at the extreme. It shows the horrifying wilderness to which the territory of exclusion, once entered, may lead; a wilderness beyond which there can only be a void, a bottomless black hole. The underclass is a vivid portrayal of the nothingness into which humans may descend, fall or be pushed; and the plight of those in the 'underclass' looks hopelessly irreversible and irreparable, gone beyond the point of no return: once there, there is no way back, one cannot return from Hades, one look will cast you back into that otherwordly darkness, as Orpheus and Euridice learned the hard – indeed, the tragic – way. This is why the underclass is found so abhorrent and repellent, for being, as Bertolt Brecht observed, *ein Bote des Unglück* (a harbinger of misfortune): the underclass reveals and brutally displays a hair-raising possibility of which we would rather stay unaware. What has happened to them might happen to any of us. If we don't try hard enough to stay afloat. And even if we try . . . To the Captain and the Doctor, Wozzeck is indeed a harbinger of misfortune, and for that reason whatever he does will be taken down and held against him; we can't forget the message – but we can unload the dread it awakes on the messenger. Wozzeck is frightening – and he cannot help it, since even if he were the most gentle, talkative and benevolent human being instead of the crestfallen, taciturn and embittered creature he is, he would still be frightening as the harbinger of frightening news.

. . . Feared, resented, humiliated

What is so frightening about Wozzeck and his ilk – *die arme Leut'* – is the Fate of which he has been, so obviously, a victim. 'Fate' is the name we give to the kinds of happenings we can neither predict nor prevent: events we neither desired nor caused. To something that 'occurred to us', not of our intention, let alone our making; to turns of fortune that descend on us like the proverbial bolt from the blue. 'Fate' frightens us precisely for being unpredictable and unpreventable. It reminds us that there are limits to what we ourselves can do to shape our lives as we would like them to be shaped; limits we can't cross, things we can't control – however earnestly we try. 'Fate' is the very epitome of the Unknown, of something we can neither explain nor understand – and this is why it is so frightening. To quote Wittgenstein one more time, 'to understand' means 'to know how to go on'; by the same token, if something happens that we don't understand, we do not know what to do; it makes us feel hapless and helpless, impotent. Being hapless is humiliating at any time, but never as much as when 'fate' strikes *individually*: when *I* am the one who has been hit, while *others around me* were bypassed by the disaster and went on as if nothing had happened. Other people seem to have managed to emerge unharmed and intact, but I've failed, abominably . . . There must therefore be something wrong with me personally, something that has invited the catastrophe, that has drawn the disaster in my direction while omitting other folk, who are obviously more clever, insightful and industrious than I am . . .

The feeling of humiliation always erodes the self-esteem and self-confidence of the humiliated, but never more severely than when humiliation is suffered alone. It is in these cases that insult is added to injury: an intimate connection between harsh fate and the victim's own, individual failings is surmised. This is why Wozzeck desperately tries to 'deindividualize' both his misery and his ineptitude, and recast them as just one example of the suffering common to the multitude of *arme Leut'*. Those who castigate and deride him attempt, on the contrary, to 'individualize' his indolence. They will not hear of *arme Leut'* and the fate they share. As desperately as Wozzeck seeks to deindividualize his misfortune, they seek to place responsibility on Wozzeck's individual shoulders. By doing so, they will perhaps manage to chase away (or at least stifle for a time) the awful premonition that emanates from the sight of Wozzeck's misfortune (the premonition that something like this may happen to them, if they stumble . . .). Wozzeck, they loudly insist, hoping to silence their own anxiety, has brought his bad luck upon himself. Through his actions or inaction he has chosen his own fate. We, however, his critics, have chosen a different kind of life, and so Wozzeck's misery cannot be visited on us. In just the same way a City of London millionaire recently tried to convince two inquisitive journalists that the disparity

between his wealth and the poverty of others was due entirely to
moral causes: 'Quite a lot of people have done well who want to
achieve, and quite a lot of people haven't done well because they
don't want to achieve.'[1] Just like that: who wants to do well, does
– who doesn't, doesn't. Doubts, premonitions, pangs of anxiety,
they are all placated, at least for a time (they will need to be put
to rest again tomorrow, and the day after tomorrow): just as the
failures of the failed are due entirely to their own volitional short-
comings, my achievements are due entirely to my own will and
determination. Just as Wozzeck must hide behind the fate of *arme
Leut'* to salvage whatever remains of his self-esteem, so the Captain
and the Doctor must strip Wozzeck's fate down to the bare bones
of individual failings to salvage whatever remains of their
self-confidence . . .

And eighty years later?

The contemporary descendants of the Captain and the Doctor, like
that millionaire from the City of London, must do the same, and
with still greater zeal and effort. Their zeal must be greater because
nowadays 'Fate' is yet more blatantly free-roaming, striking at
random, and with more devastating effect, than it seemed to be
in the aftermath of the World War believed to be 'the war to end
all wars' (for an abominably short time, as it soon transpired), a
war that was to usher in times of peace, rising well-being, more
chances and less misery for everybody. If Berg's generation lived
by the dream and the hope of imminent existential security, the
generations filling the house of the Bavarian State Opera in 2008
live with the conviction of lifelong, permanent, and perhaps incurable insecurity. In some convoluted sense, the musings of the
Captain and the Doctor have proved to be right, at least in the
long run – a sort of self-fulfilling prophecy: fate, indeed, seems
now to have been privatized. It strikes individuals, all too often
bypassing their next-door neighbours. Its itinerary is no less irregular than it ever was, but the frequency of blows being delivered
feels more regular (monotonous, even routine) than ever before.
It is just as in *Big Brother*, officially described as, and commonly
believed to be, a '*reality* show', in which, come what may, one of
the protagonists, just one, simply must be excluded (voted out)

from the team every week – and the only thing unknown is who it will be this week and whose turn will come a week later. Exclusion is in the nature of things, an undetachable aspect of being-in-the-world, a 'law of nature', so to speak – and so to rebel against it makes no sense. The only issue worthy of being thought about, and intensely, is how to stave off the prospect of *me* being the one excluded in the next week's round. No one can claim to be immune to the meanderings of Fate. No one can really feel insured against the threat of being excluded. Most of us have either already tasted the bitterness of exclusion, or suspected that we might have to – at some undisclosed time in the future. It seems that only a few of us can swear that they are immune to Fate, and we are allowed to suspect that eventually most of those few will be proved wrong. Only a few can hope that they'll never learn how it feels to go through Wozzeck's kind of experience (*Erlebnisse*!). One aspect of his experience in particular: how it feels to be snubbed and to suffer humiliation.

It needs to be said, however, that the meaning and the main cause of humiliation has altered since Berg's opera was scripted (and so, in a sense, the meaning has been changed of '*arme Leute*', the people who have reason to complain of deprivation). Today, the stake of cut-throat individual competition, including the lottery of exclusion, is no longer physical survival (at least in the affluent part of the planet, and at least currently and 'until further notice') – not the satisfaction of the primary biological needs which the survival instinct demands. Neither is it the right to self-assertion, to setting one's own objectives and deciding what kind of life one would prefer to live, since, on the contrary, the exercise of such rights is assumed to be every individual's duty. Moreover, it is now an axiom that whatever happens to an individual can only be the consequence of exercising such rights, or of an abominable failure or sinful refusal to exercise them. Whatever happens to an individual will be retrospectively interpreted as another confirmation of the individual's sole and inalienable responsibility for their individual plight: adversities as much as successes.

Cast as individuals by decree of history, we are now encouraged to actively seek 'social recognition' for what has been already pre-interpreted as our individual choices: namely, the forms of life which we, individuals, are practising (whether by deliberate choice or by default). 'Social recognition' means acceptance, by 'others who matter', that a form of life practised by a particular individual is worthy and decent, and that on this ground the individual in question deserves the respect owed and normally offered to all deserving, worthy and decent people.

Dreaming of recognition, fearing its denial . . .

The alternative to social recognition is the denial of dignity: humiliation. In the recent definition by Dennis Smith, an 'act is humiliating if it forcefully overrides or contradicts the claim that particular individuals . . . are making about who they are and where and how they fit in'.[2] In other words, if the individual is, explicitly or implicitly, denied the recognition which she or he expected for the person she or he is and/or the kind of life she or he lives; and if she or he is refused the entitlements that would have been made available or would have continued to be available following such recognition. A person feels humiliated when she or he is 'brutally shown, by words, actions or events, that they cannot be what they think they are . . . Humiliation is the experience of being unfairly, unreasonably and unwillingly pushed down, held down, held back or pushed out.'[3]

That feeling breeds resentment. In a society of individuals like ours, the pain, peevishness and rancour of having been humiliated are arguably the most venomous and implacable variety of resentment a person may feel, and the most common and prolific cause of conflict, dissent, rebellion and a thirst for revenge. Denial of recognition, refusal of respect and threat of exclusion have replaced exploitation and discrimination as the formulae most commonly used to explain and justify the grudges individuals might bear towards society, or to the sections or aspects of society to which they are directly exposed (personally or through the media) and which they thereby experience (whether at first or second hand).

The shame of humiliation breeds self-contempt and self-hatred, which tend to overwhelm us once we realize how weak, indeed impotent, we are when we attempt to hold fast to the identity of our choice, to our place in the community we respect and cherish, and to the kind of life we dearly wish to be ours and remain ours for a long time to come – once we find out how frail our identity is, how vulnerable and unsteady are our past achievements, and how uncertain our future must be in view of the magnitude of the daily challenges we face. That shame, and so the self-hatred too, rise as the proof of our impotence accumulates – and as the sense of humiliation deepens as a result.

Self-hatred, however, is an unbearably harrowing, and unendurable state to be in, and to stay in: self-hatred needs, and desperately seeks, an outlet – it must be channelled away from our inner self, which it may otherwise seriously damage or even destroy. The chain leading from uncertainty, through feelings of impotence, shame and humiliation, to self-disgust, self-loathing and self-hatred, therefore ends up in the search of a culprit 'out there, in the world'; of that someone, still unknown and unnamed, invisible or disguised, who conspires against my (our) dignity and well-being, and makes me (us) suffer that excruciating pain of humiliation. A discovery and unmasking of that someone is badly needed, because we need a target on which to unleash our pent-up anger. The pains must be avenged, though it is far from clear in whose direction. . . . Exploding self-hatred hits targets, just as Wozzeck did, at random – mostly those closest to hand, though not necessarily those most responsible for one's fall, humiliation and misery.

We need someone to hate because we need someone to blame for our abominable and unendurable condition and the defeats we suffer when we try to improve it and make it more secure. We need that someone in order to unload (and so hopefully mitigate) the devastating sense of our own unworthiness. For that unloading to be successful, however, the whole operation needs to thoroughly cover up all traces of a *personal* vendetta. The intimate link between the perception of the loathsomeness and hatefulness of the chosen target, and our frustration in search of an outlet, must be kept secret. In whatever way hatred was conceived, we prefer to explain its presence, to others around us and to ourselves, by our will to defend the good and noble things which they, those malicious and despicable people, denigrate and conspire against; we will struggle to prove that the reason for hating them, and our determination to get rid of them, have been caused (and justified) by our wish to make sure that an orderly, civilized society survives. *We will insist that we hate because we want the world to be free of hatred.*

It does not agree, perhaps, with the logic of things, but it does chimes well with the logic of emotions, that the underclass and others like them – homeless refugees, the uprooted, the 'not belonging', the asylum-seekers-but-not-finders, the *sans papiers* – tend to attract our resentment and aversion. All those people seem to have been made to the measure of our fears. They are walking illustrations to which our nightmares wrote the captions. They are the living traces (sediments, signs, embodiments) of all those mysterious forces, commonly called 'globalization', we hold responsible for the threat of being forcefully torn away from the place we love (in country or society) and pushed onto a road with few if any signposts and no known destination. They represent formidable forces, admittedly, but they themselves are weak and can be defeated with the weapons we have. *Summa summarum*, they are ideally suited for the role of an effigy in which those forces, indomitable and beyond our reach, can be burned, even if only by proxy.

The leitmotif, composed by Alban Berg, introduced by Wozzeck with the words *Wir arme Leut*, scripted by Georg Büchner, signals the inability of the opera's characters to transcend their situation; an inability which the characters on stage share with the crowds in the audience. Romantic artists wished to see the universe in a drop of water. Wozzeck's detractors as much as Wozzeck himself might be but drops of water, but if we try we can see in them if not the universe, than surely our *Lebenswelt* . . .

11

Sociology: whence and whither?

More than a hundred and twenty years ago, Albion Small opined that sociology was born of the modern zeal to make society better. No one has since managed to convincingly refute the correctness of his observation. So much time later I suggest that, looking back, we can say that sociology was not just 'born of', but lived for most of its life by that modern zeal to make society better (if not for any other reason, then surely for the conviction we all share that a society that contains sociology is better than a society that does not). Wishing to make society better was a constant, invariable factor in the sociological equation. But if this is indeed the case, sociology has no history – only a chronicle; or at least it wouldn't have a history were it not that the meaning of 'making better' has changed – together with the content and objects of that 'modern zeal' . . . I believe that any decent textbook of the 'history of sociology' must focus on the evolution of the meaning sociologists inserted, whether by design or default, but always following the twists and turns of that 'modern zeal', into the idea of 'making society better'.

As newcomers applying for an entry permit to the land of academia quite a few centuries after the laws of that land had been written up for insiders to obey and for false pretenders and illegal immigrants to stay outside, sociologists needed to demonstrate their willingness and ability to behave as the laws of the land demanded: to play the game the laws of the land prescribed and to play it by the rules they had set. The game to be played was called 'science'.

Different from each other as the two most famous of the applicants were in virtually every detail of their applications, so different indeed as to fail to recognize and acknowledge being partners or collaborators in the same métier, Weber and Durkheim agreed on one point: the upstart, the arriviste, they represented firmly intended to play the only game in the land. That game being science, sociology was and intended to remain a scientific endeavour. Durkheim, inspired by Auguste Comte's vision of universal precepts of the scientific attitude, the same for all, set out to prove that the sociological sector of science wouldn't be any different in its purpose and behavioural code from the established segments – that is, the segments whose scientific credentials were no longer questioned (whether biology, physics or demography), all trying to pierce through the mystery of reality and register the laws obeyed by the genuine, tough and indomitable realities, the unshakeable 'facts of the matter'. For his part, Weber, who had grown and been groomed inside the German tradition of *Geistes-* or *Kultur-wissenschaften,* admitted that the sociological variety of science would be different from the ways of doing science practised elsewhere; yet he insisted that this did not testify to its inferiority, but on the contrary showed its greater scientific potential, in that the *understanding* which sociology was after was bound to stay staunchly beyond the reach of those sciences that were barred from using words like 'intention', 'purpose' or 'goals', and had thereby been compelled to settle for mere *explanation*: for composing inventories of causes. But neither of the two pioneers allowed any doubt as to the scientific status of sociology, let alone any questioning of its scientific status being a *sine qua non*, a legitimate and fully justified as well as praiseworthy condition of naturalization in the land of academia. So what did it mean in practice?

Since its birth (that unsurprisingly coincided with the absconding of Europe's monotheistic God), the science's self-portrait was painted using a monotheistic palette. Memorably, Jahve – that archetype of absolute authority by which all later aspirers to every and any variety of commanding stature measured their ambitions – 'answered Job out of the tempest' (note that by speaking, unlike Job, 'out of the tempest', Jahve pre-empted Job's chance of responding with a comparable degree of authority):

Who is this whose ignorant words
Cloud my design in darkness?
Brace yourself and stand up like a man;
I will ask questions, and you shall answer
. . .
only to ask in turn:
Should he who argues with God answer back?
                              (Job 38: 2–3; 40: 2)

Asked 'out of the tempest', that last question was of course purely rhetorical: Jahve had left Job in no doubt about its status, when summarizing his lengthy lecture by reminding Job that he, Jahve, and he only, 'looks down to all creatures, even the highest' (Job 41: 34). To which Job, so voluble and outspoken on other occasions, found no answer except 'therefore I melt away; I repent in dust and ashes' (Job 42: 6).

Well, *hier*, as the Germans would say, *liegt der Hund begraben* – here's the rub. The principal stake in the war waged by the monotheists against their polytheistic adversaries is the entitlement to soliloquy. Monotheism equals monologue. The ascendancy of the *monologue* and the disqualification of its opposite and declared enemy, the *dialogue* (or more to the point the *polylogue*), means a strict and irreversible division of status between 'subject' and 'object', or 'doing' and 'suffering'; it means therefore the legitimacy of only one voice, coupled with a disqualification of all the rest of the voices as illegitimate; it means the right to stifle, silence, declare out of court all except one voice – or to ignore those other voices in the event that silencing them proves not entirely successful. Ideally, it means the achieving by that one voice of the prerogative to render all 'other voices' inadmissible in the court of law, and so purely and simply inaudible – this being sufficient to make all further argumentation redundant, if not an act of profanation and a sin of blasphemy.

Nuclear physicists, biologists, geologists or astronomers have no difficulty in obtaining such a prerogative, and thereby such a monotheistic status. They need do nothing at all to assure it; the uncontestable authority of their pronouncements on the conduct of electrons, organic cells, mineral deposits and distant galaxies is a priori assured by the sheer impossibility of their objects voicing their disagreement in the language in which the scientists' judgements were made. And if the wordless conduct of the objects of their study belies the expectations which their judgements imply, it is again up to them, the scientists, and them only, to recycle what they have seen into the 'facts of the matter' as seen by and in science.

Sociologists' bid for scientific status inevitably calls for the *construction*, by their own efforts and with the help of instruments (stratagems, contraptions, expedients) of their own invention and design, of a state of affairs which nuclear physicists have the luxury of taking *for granted*. Our sociologists' objects of study are not dumb by nature. For us to retain our monotheistic/monologist status and to secure the sovereign authority of our pronouncements, the objects to which our pronouncements refer need first to be made *dumb* (as Gaston Bachelard, the great historian of science, observed: the first truly scientific book was one that did not start with reference to a mundane and universally shared human experience, like a lid jumping on a pot of boiling water or air refreshing after a storm, but with a quotation from a study by another scientist). The dumbness of our objects, which happen to be fellow human beings armed with their mundane wisdom called 'doxa' or 'common sense', needs to be *our accomplishment*. It needs to be *achieved*. But how?

Essentially, by one of two conceivable strategies: through limiting our pronouncements on the (human, all too human) objects of our study to things or events which our objects, having no personal experience of them and so no chance of scrutinizing their veracity, are obliged to take on faith (such as, for instance, huge volumes of 'data' that would not have been brought into being unless they had been lavishly financed by research grants and stipends); and/or through wrapping our judgements in a language which the objects of our study are unable to comprehend, and in which they couldn't therefore respond, even in the unlikely event they wished or dared to do so. The two strategies have a common denominator: they both aim at *preventing*, in our relations with the objects of our study, that 'fusion of horizons' which Hans-Georg Gadamer viewed as the necessary condition of all meaningful, undisturbed and effective communication.

Unlike electrons or positrons, humans are not Descartes-style passive objects of cognition, the subject's constructs, owing to the cognizing subject all the sense they may gain or be assigned; but our bid for a scientific status is bound to be in the last account an intention to make them into precisely such passive objects, or at least to treat them as if they were. Our bid for a scientific status presupposes a *unilateral break in communication*. In practice, such a bid equals a willingness to voluntarily forfeit the cognitive chance offered by our shared humanity, in exchange for scientific, that is monologist, status for our narratives: to obtain by hook or by crook and by our own ingenuity what nature offered our colleagues from the 'natural' sciences on a plate, ready for consumption and enjoyment.

Expropriation being the other side of appropriation, Weber and Durkheim had to do, and did, their best to denigrate and devalue *avant la lettre* whatever other human beings, recast for that purpose as 'non-professionals', might say to make sense of their own deeds. Durkheim's blunt verdict (in *Les règles de la méthode sociologique*) was that the representations of facts 'which we have been able to make in the course of our life, have been made uncritically and unmethodically' (that is, not in the way we would proceed *qua* sociologists) and for that reason 'are devoid of scientific value and must be discarded'. Short of the scientifically endorsed method, humans are only capable of 'confused, fleeting, subjective' impressions. With the possible exception of mathematics, Durkheim reminds us, 'every object of science is a thing'. What follows is that, in order to be admitted into the scientific observatory or the laboratory, humans need first to be truncated, curtailed and reduced to the modality of things. B. F. Skinner would later draw the proper conclusion from Durkheim's recommendation and declare that everything that goes on inside human heads is shut forever inside 'black boxes', impenetrable to the scientific eye and so of no relevance or interest to science. Paul Lazarsfeld will apologize for sociology's sloth and ineptitude: 'Sociology is not yet at the stage where it can provide a safe basis for social engineering . . . It took the natural sciences 250 years between Galileo and the beginning of the industrial revolution before they had a major effect upon the history of the world. Empirical social research has a history of three or four decades.' While in the view of Otto Neurath, hugely influential in his time as a radical advocate of 'here as there, in *Kulturwissenschaften* as in *Naturwissenschaften*', 'sociology ought to rest on a materialist basis, and that means to treat men just like other sciences treat animals, plants, or stones. Sociology is *eine Realwissenschaft*, in the same way as, say, astronomy. Populations are like galaxies of stars more closely linked to each other than to other stars.' Weber would not go the whole hog with Durkheim, let alone Skinner or Neurath; he would not wish the objects of sociological science to be as reduced as they intended. Weber's ambitions reached further: having refused to dismiss the sentient, self-guided (even if testifying to self-deception and/or being duped) aspect of human beings, he wished to secure for sociologists an entitlement to soliloquy not only in relation to the *behavioural* aspects of human actions, but also in relation to their admittedly *subjective* aspects like motives, reasons, purposes – pointing out that 'in the great majority of cases actual action goes on in a state of inarticulate half-consciousness or actual unconsciousness of its subjective meaning'.

> The 'conscious motives' may well, even to the actor himself, conceal the various 'motives' and 'repressions' which constitute the real driving forces of the action. Thus . . . even subjectively honest self-analysis has only a relative value. Then it is the task of the sociologist to be aware of this motivational situation and to describe and analyse it, even though it has not actually been concretely part of the conscious 'intention' of the actor.

In other words, humans can be admitted into the field of scientific scrutiny also in their capacity of intentional, motivated beings – though on condition of renouncing, or being deprived of, their right to judge what their intentions and motives really are. One thing which Weber could not forgive Georg Simmel (his contemporary refused academic office for all but the three last years of his life, and even then thanks to the conscription of a good many teaching staff to the killing fields of the Great War) was his original sin of putting the inferior 'conscious motives' of actors on a level with the superior renderings of their intentions by their scientific analysts – if not confusing their distinct modalities altogether, instead of keeping them in uncompromising opposition to each other.

But enough of retelling the story which surely must sound boringly familiar to most people gathered in this room. I invoked that story solely in order to suggest that the plea for recognition of its scientific status was one of the causes of sociology landing in the role of handmaiden to Managerial Reason (or rather, in its own

outspoken intention, of matron of the maidservants' quarters).
That Reason, which had its cradle in Francis Bacon's House of
Solomon, spent its apprenticeship years in Jeremy Bentham's
Panopticon, and had already in our lifetime settled into the innumerable factory buildings haunted by the ghosts of Frederick
Winslow Taylor's 'time and motion measurements', by the spectre
of Henry Ford's conveyor belt, and by the phantom of Le
Corbusier's idea of home as a 'machine for living'. That Reason
assumed that the variety and divergence of human intentions and
preferences were just temporary irritants, bound to be pushed out
of the way of the order-building enterprise through a skilful
manipulation of behavioural probabilities via a proper arrangement of external settings and through rendering impotent and
irrelevant all features resistant to such manipulation.

In the late 1930s, in a book aptly named *The Managerial
Revolution*, James Burnham suggested that managers, originally
hired by the owners of machines with a brief to drill, discipline
and supervise their operators in order to elicit their maximum
efforts, had taken over the real power from their employers –
owners or stockholders. Managers had been hired and paid for
their services because day-to-day management of sloppy and
essentially unwilling and distastefully resentful labourers was an
awkward and cumbersome task, a chore which the owners of
machinery did not relish doing themselves and would willingly
pay to get rid of. No wonder the owners used their wealth to buy
services they hoped would release them from the unrewarding and
unwanted burden. As it transpired shortly afterwards, however, it
was precisely that function of 'managing' – forcing or cajoling
other people to do, day in day out, something they would rather
not do, and in the end recycling necessities into character traits
– that was the real power that counted. The hired managers turned
into the real bosses. Power was now in the hands of those who
managed other people's actions, rather than of those who owned
the 'means of production'. Managers turned out to be the genuine
power-holders; a turn of events which Karl Marx, in his vision of
an imminent confrontation between capital and labour, did not
anticipate.

Managing, bequeathed in its original sense from the times when
a profitable industrial process was conceived after the pattern
of a homeostatic machine going through predesigned repetitive

motions and kept on a steady, immutable course, was indeed a chore. It required meticulous regimentation and close 'panoptical' supervision. It needed the imposition of a monotonous routine bound to stultify the creative impulses of *both* the managed and the managers. It generated boredom and a constantly seething resentment that threatened to self-combust into open conflict. It was also an exceedingly costly and indeed wasteful way of 'getting things done': instead of enlisting the non-regimented potentials of hired labour in the service of the job, it used precious resources to stifle them, excise them and keep them out of mischief. All in all, day-to-day management was not a kind of task which resourceful people, people in power, were likely to relish and cherish: they would not perform it a moment longer than they had to, and given the power resources at their disposal they could not be expected to put off that moment for long. And they did not.

The current 'great transformation mark two' (to invoke Karl Polanyi's memorable phrase), the emergence of a widely lauded and welcome 'experience economy' drawing its fuel from the *totality* of the resources of the personality, warts and all, signals that the moment of the 'emancipation of managers from the burden of managing' has arrived. Using James Burnham's terms, one could describe it as the 'Managerial Revolution mark two'; though this time there has been little or no change in the composition of the incumbents of office and power. What has happened – is happening – is more a coup d'état than a revolution: a proclamation from the top that the old game is abandoned and new rules of the game are in force. The people who prompted and saw through the revolution remained at the helm and if anything settled in their offices yet more securely than before. This revolution was initiated and conducted in the name of *adding* to their power: further strengthening their grip, and immunizing their domination against the resentment and rebellion which the form of their domination used to generate, before the revolution. After the second managerial revolution, the power of the managers was reinforced and made well-nigh invulnerable – through cutting off most of the restraining and otherwise inconvenient strings previously attached to it.

On the crest of their second revolution, the managers banished the pursuit of routine and invited the forces of spontaneity to occupy the now vacant room. They refused to manage; instead, they now demand that the residents, on the threat of eviction, *self-manage*. The right to extend the lease of the office has been made subject to recurrent competition: after each round, the most playful and the best performing win the next term of lease, though without a guarantee, or even an increased likelihood, of emerging unscathed from the next test. On the walls of the banqueting suite of the 'experience economy' the reminder that 'you are as good as your last success' (but not as your last but one) has replaced the inscription, 'Mene, Tekel, Upharsin' ('counted, weighed, allocated'). Favouring subjectivity, playfulness and performativity, the organizations of the 'experience economy' era had to, wished to, and did prohibit long-term planning and the accumulation of merits. This indeed may keep its residents constantly on the move – in the feverish search for ever new evidence that they are still welcome.

Two birds have been hit with one stone. First, a complete or at least partial emancipation of power-holders from the unpleasant and so resented aspects of the managerial position. And an opening to exploitation (direct or indirect) of the vast areas of employees' selves or personalities, hitherto left outside the package deal obtained by managers when 'buying labour'. Self-managing, 'hived off' or 'outsourced' employees can be relied upon to reach for resources the managers could not reach, to deploy parts of their selves kept off-limits to bosses in traditional labour contracts, and not to count the hours spent in serving the aims of the employing company. Such new-type employees may also be relied on to control, make harmless and even turn profitable those parts of their selves which might have been potentially counterproductive or disruptive, or at least difficult to tame and disable, had they been admitted to the shared workplace under the rule and direct responsibility of the managers.

My time here is barely sufficient to sketch even in the broadest of outlines the tendencies of the emergent 'experience economy', and a managerial style that, in the words of Nigel Thrift, 'conveys the message of volatility, fluidity, flexibility and short life-span'. Besides, the history of organizations in the liquid modern era is yet to begin to be lived through; to write up its story will take much longer. What I am prepared to risk is only a depressingly and shamefully brief survey of the impact already made and likely to go on being made by the 'Managerial Revolution mark two' on the status and prospects of what is our only, the sociological, vocation.

The first impact is the widespread, even if deceptive, feeling that sociology has lost its access to the public arena, together with the demand for its services. The feeling is deceptive, I suggest, because the 'public arena' is tacitly identified with its one-time form (institutionalized, for instance, by warfare-and welfare bureaucracies), and its own 'services' with the kind of knowledge sociology was trained and volunteered to supply at the time of its scientific temptations. The feeling is also deceptive for another, yet more seminal reason: the 'Managerial Revolution mark two', just one aspect of the 'Great Transformation mark two', in fact assigns to sociology a public role of unprecedented significance and offers us (though unintentionally and inadvertently) a constituency of an unprecedented size. There has been, I would argue, no other moment in history when so many people have needed so much of such vital goods for sociology to deliver.

Thus the second impact is the urgent (even if, for the time being, far from fully acknowledged and recognized) need to reorientate the self-definition, the purpose or mission, and the strategy of sociology. For more than half a century of its recent history, seeking to be of service to managerial reason, sociology struggled to establish itself as a *science/technology of unfreedom*: as a design workshop for social settings meant to resolve in theory, but most importantly in practice, what Talcott Parsons memorably articulated as 'the Hobbesian question': how to induce, force or indoctrinate human beings, blessed or cursed with the ambiguous gift of free will, to be normatively guided and to routinely follow manipulable, yet predictable courses of action; or how to reconcile free will with a willingness to submit to other people's will, thereby lifting the tendency to 'voluntary servitude', noted and anticipated by la Boètie at the threshold of the modern era, to the rank of the supreme principle of social organization. In short, how to make people have the *will* to do what they *must* . . .

In our society, individualized by a decree of fate aided and abetted by the second managerial revolution, sociology faces the exciting and exhilarating chance of turning for a change into a *science/technology of freedom*: a science of the ways and means through which the individuals-by-decree and *de jure* of liquid modern times may be lifted to the rank of individuals-*by-choice* and *de facto*. Or, to take a leaf from Jeffrey Alexander's call to arms: sociology's future, at least its immediate future, lies in an effort to reincarnate and to re-establish itself as *cultural politics in the service of human freedom.*

As a result of all that, the kind of sociology that dominated academia for many decades, a sociology made to the measure of the demands and expectations of the managerial reason of yore has found itself out of a job. There are few if any buyers left for its staple products. Hence the blues ... Some distinguished American sociologists complain of having lost contact with the 'public sphere', and wonder whether that link can be restored. But let's be clear about it: it is only one particular sector of the 'public sphere' that dissolved, retreated from the 'human engineering' business or withdrew its interest. Present-day fears are an outcome of sociology one-sidedly overspecializing in running an industry that has lost, or is fast losing, its clientele. It was, however, only one of the possible ways of doing sociology – and not, let me confess, a kind whose demise I personally would be inclined to mourn and bewail.

I'd suggest that sociology has little choice but to follow, now as ever, the track of the changing world; the alternative would be nothing less than a loss of relevance. But I'd suggest as well that the particular 'no choice' quandary that we face today should be anything but a cause for despair. Quite the contrary. In our short history, yet a history rich in crises and fateful choices, no nobler, more elevated and morally laudable mission was ever imposed on our discipline with such force, while simultaneously being made similarly realistic – not at any other of the times which, as Hegel suggested two centuries ago, it is the prime destination and perennial vocation of humanity to catch.

One seminal function and duty that, in the course of recent liquid modern individualization, was dropped from the heights of an 'imagined totality' into the cauldron of (to borrow Anthony Giddens's term) individually conducted 'life politics' has been, to all practical intents and purposes, the task of truth validation and meaning production. This does not mean, of course, that the truths for individual validation and the raw stuff from which individuals mould their meanings have stopped being *socially* supplied; but it does mean that they now tend to be media-and-shop supplied, rather than being imposed through communal command;

and that they are calculated to *seduce clients* rather than *compel subordinates*. The task of choice-making, complete with the responsibility for the consequences of choice, now falls and needs to be carried on individuals' shoulders.

This is a totally new ball game, as Americans used to say. It has its promises – not the least the chance of shifting morality from conformity to ethical commands to an unconditionally individual responsibility for the well-being of others. But it is also filled with dangers, and augurs a life full of risks. It casts individuals (and that means all of us) in a state of acute, and in all probability incurable, underdetermination and uncertainty. As views memorized and skills acquired are poor and all too often misleading or even treacherous guides to action, and as the knowledge available transcends the individual capacity to assimilate it, whereas the assimilated fraction usually falls far short of what is required by an understanding of the situation (the knowledge of how to go on, that is) – the condition of frailty, transience and contingency has become for the duration, and perhaps for a very long time to come, the natural human habitat. And so it is with this sort of human experience that sociology needs to engage in a continuous dialogue.

I'd say that the twin roles which we, sociologists, are called on to perform in that dialogue are those of the *defamiliarizing the familiar* and *familiarizing* (taming, domesticating) *the unfamiliar*. Both roles demand skilfulness in opening to scrutiny the net of links, influences and dependencies which is too vast to be thoroughly surveyed, fully scanned and grasped with the resources supplied by individual experience. They also demand the kinds of skills best caught in the phrase of the English novelist E. M. Forster, 'only connect': skilfulness in reconnecting and making whole again the notoriously fragmented and disconnected images of the *Lebenswelt* – the world lived in our times from episode to episode, and individually lived through, at individual risk and with individual benefit in mind. Last though not least, they call for skills in uncovering the 'doxa' (the knowledge we think with but not about), pulling it out of the murky depths of the subconscious, and so enabling and setting in motion a process of perpetual critical scrutiny, and perhaps even conscious control over its contents, by those who are thus far unaware of possessing it and of unwittingly using it. In other words, they call for the art of *dialogue*.

To be sure, dialogue is a difficult art. It means engaging in conversation with the intention of jointly clarifying the issues, rather than having them one's own way; of multiplying voices, rather than reducing their number; of widening the set of possibilities, rather than aiming at a wholesale consensus (that relic of monotheistic dreams stripped of politically incorrect coercion); of jointly pursuing understanding, instead of aiming at the other's defeat; and all in all being animated by the wish to keep the conversation going, rather than by a desire to grind it to a halt. Mastering that art is terribly time-consuming, though far less time-intensive than practising it. Neither of the two undertakings, nor the mastering and practising together, promise to make our life easier. But they do promise to make our lives more exciting and rewarding to us, as well as more useful to our fellow humans – and to transform our professional chores into a continuous and neverending voyage of discovery.

Not to steal more of your time, that most precious resource notorious for its supply being in inverse proportion to demand, I finish my speech. Much has been left out of my speech that shouldn't have been, and I am sure that you've found in it many more questions than answers. But here you are: this is how it is going to be from now on, in case we decide to embark on the voyage whose itinerary I have tried, ineptly, to anticipate. What remains to be said, then, is *bon voyage*!

Notes

Introduction

1   This and the following quotations come from David Gonzalez, 'From margins of society to centre of the tragedy', *New York Times*, 2 Sept. 2005.
2   See my *Wasted Lives*, Polity, 2004.

Chapter 1   From the agora to the marketplace

I am grateful for permission to draw on material here from my article 'Ot agory k rynku – i kuda potom?' *Svobodnaya Mysl* 8 (2009).

1   Albert O. Hirschman, *Exit, Voice, and Loyalty: Responses to Decline in Firms, Organizations, and States*, Harvard University Press, 1970.
2   T. H. Marshall, *Citizenship and Social Class and Other Essays*, Cambridge University Press, 1950.
3   See among others of John Kenneth Galbraith's works his *Culture of Contentment*, Houghton Mifflin, 1992.
4   Oliver James, 'Selfish capitalism is bad for our mental health', *Guardian*, 3 Jan. 2008.
5   Laurent Bonelli, 'L'antiterrorisme en France, un systeme liberticide', *Le Monde*, 11 Sept. 2008.
6   Jacques Attali, *La Voie humaine*, Fayard, 2004.
7   Joseph Stiglitz, 'Trade imbalances', *Guardian*, 15 Aug. 2003.

Chapter 2   Requiem for communism

I am grateful for permission to draw on material here from my contribution to *Thesis Eleven* 3 (2009).

1   Daniel Bell, *The Cultural Contradictions of Capitalism*, Heinemann, 1976, p. 4.
2   Leonidas Donskis, *Troubled Identity and the Modern World*, Palgrave, 2009, p. 139.
3   See F. Feher, Agnes Heller and G. Markus, *Dictatorship over Needs*, Blackwell, 1983.
4   See Vladimir Voinovich, *Moscow 2042*, Harvest Books, 1987 (Russian original 1986).
5   See Amelia Gentleman, 'Indian election: challenge of narrowing shaming gulf between wealth and want', *Guardian*, 12 May 2009.
6   See Larry Elliott and Polly Curtis, 'Gap between rich and poor widest since 60s', *Guardian*, 8 May 2009.

Chapter 3   The fate of social inequality in liquid modern times

1   Michael Crozier, The *Bureaucratic Phenomenon*, Tavistock, 1964.
2   Nigel Thrift, 'The rise of soft capitalism', *Cultural Values* (Apr. 1997), p. 52.
3   See Glenn Firebaugh, *The New Geography of Global Income Inequality*, Harvard University Press, 2003.

Chapter 4   Strangers are dangers . . . Are they indeed?

1   See Ulrich Beck, *Risiko Gesellschaft. Auf dem Weg in einere andere Moderne*, Suhrkamp, 1986; here quoted from Mark Ritter's translation, *Risk Society*, Sage, 1992, p. 137.
2   Cf. Nathaniel Herzberg and Cécile Prieur, 'Lionel Jospin et le "piège" sécuritaire', *Le Monde*, 5–6 May 2002.
3   Quoted by Donald G. McNeil Jr, 'Politicians pander to fear of crime', *New York Times*, 5–6 May 2002.
4   As noted by the narrator in Jonathan Littell, *Les Bienveillantes*, Gallimard, 2006, here quoted from Charlotte Mandell's English translation, *The Kindly Ones*, Chatto & Windus, 2009, p. 390.
5   Teresa Caldeira, 'Fortified enclaves: the new urban segregation', *Public Culture* 8(2) (1996), pp. 303–28.
6   Nan Elin, 'Shelter from the storm, or form follows fear and vice versa', in Nan Elin (ed.), *Architecture of Fear*, Princeton Architectural Press, 1997, pp. 13, 26.
7   Steven Flusty, 'Building paranoia', in Elin, *Architecture of Fear*, pp. 48–52.

8   Richard Sennett, *The Uses of Disorder: Personal Identity and City Life*, Faber & Faber, 1996, pp. 39, 42.

9   Oscar Newman, *Defensible Space: People and Design in the Violent City*, London: Architectural Press, 1973.

10 Anna Minton, *Ground Control: Fear and Happiness in the Twenty-First-Century City*, Penguin, 2009, p. 171.

11 See Jane Jacobs, *The Death and Life of Great American Cities*, Random House, 1961.

Chapter 6   Privacy, secrecy, intimacy, human bonds – and other collateral casualties of liquid modernity

I am grateful for permission to draw on material here from my chapter 'Privacy, secrecy, intimacy, human bonds, utopia – and other collateral casualties of liquid modernity', in Harry Blatterer, Pauline Johnson and Maria R. Markus (eds.), *Modern Privacy: Shifting Boundaries, New Forms*, Palgrave Macmillan, 2010.

1   See Georg Simmel, 'Zur Psychologie der Mode. Soziologische Studie', in Simmel, *Gesamtausgabe*, Suhrkamp, 1992, vol. 5.

Chapter 7   Luck and the individualization of remedies

I am grateful for permission to draw on material here from my 'Sorte e individualizzazione dei rimedi', in Michelina Borsari (ed.), *Sulla Fortuna, Paginette del Festival Filosofia*, published by the editor 2010.

Chapter 8   Seeking in modern Athens an answer to the ancient Jerusalem question

I am grateful for permission to draw on material here from my article 'Seeking in modern Athens an answer to the ancient Jerusalem question', *Theory, Culture & Society* 26(1) (2010): 71–91.

1   Carl Schmitt, *Politische Theologie. Vier Kapitel zur Lehre von der Souveränität*, Duncker & Humboldt, 1922, here quoted from George Schwab's translation, *Political Theology*, University of Chicago Press, 1985, pp. 36, 10, emphasis added.

2   See Mikhail Bakhtin, *Rabelais and His World*, MIT Press, 1968 (Russian original 1965). Also Ken Hirschkop's apt summary in 'Fear and democracy: an essay on Bakhtin's theory of carnival', *Associations* 1 (1997), pp. 209–34.

3 Carl Schmitt, *Theorie des Partisanen, Zwischenbemerkung zum Begriff des Politischen*, Duncker & Humboldt, 1963, p. 80. See the discussion in Giorgio Agamben, *Homo Sacer: Sovereign Power and Bare Life*, Stanford University Press, 1998, p. 137.
4 Schmitt, *Political Theology*, pp. 19–21, emphasis added. See discussion in Agamben, *Homo Sacer*, pp. 15ff.
5 Agamben, *Homo Sacer*, p. 18, emphasis added.
6 Susan Neiman, *Evil in Modern Thought: An Alternative History of Philosophy*, Princeton University Press, 2002; Jean-Pierre Dupuy, *Petite métaphysique des tsunamis*, Seuil, 2005.
7 Jean-Jacques Rousseau, 'Lettre à Monsieur de Voltaire', in *Oeuvres complètes*, Pléiade, 1959, vol, 4, p. 1062.
8 Neiman, *Evil in Modern Thought*, p. 230, emphasis added.
9 Ibid., pp. 240, 281.
10 In other words, the unavoidable evil was suffered by the innocent and the guilty alike.
11 Ernst-Wolfgang Böckenförde, *Recht, Staat, Freiheit*, Suhrkamp, 1991, p. 112.
12 See Jan-Werner Müller, *A Dangerous Mind: Carl Schmitt in Postwar European Thought*, Yale University Press, 2003, pp. 4–5.
13 Schmitt, *Political Theology*, p. 37.
14 Ibid., p. 48.
15 Carl Schmitt, *The Concept of the Political*, trans. George Schwab (from *Der Begriff des Politischen*), University of Chicago Press, 2007, p. 26.
16 Ibid., p. 27.
17 See Beck, *Risk Society*, p. 137.
18 See *USA Today*, 11 June 2002, particularly 'Al-Qaeda operative tipped off plot', 'US: dirty bomb plot foiled' and 'Dirty bomb plot: "The future is here, I'm afraid"'.
19 Sidney Blumenthal, 'Bush's war on professionals', Salon.com, 5 Jan. 2006, at www.salon.com/opinion/blumenthal/2006/01/05/spying/index.html?x.
20 Bob Herbert, 'America the fearful', *New York Times*, 15 May 2006, p. 25.
21 Henry A. Giroux, 'Beyond the biopolitics of disposability: rethinking neoliberalism in the new gilded age', *Social Identities* 14(5) (Sept. 2008), pp. 587–620.
22 McNeil, 'Politicians pander to fear of crime', as cited above.
23 See Walter Benjamin, 'On the concept of History', in *Selected Writings*, ed. Howard Eiland and Michael W. Jennings, Harvard University Press, 2003, vol. 4.

24 See Giorgio Agamben, *Stato di eccezione*, Bollati Boringhieri, 2003;
    here quoted from the English translation by Kevin Attell, *State of
    Exception*, University of Chicago Press, 2005, pp. 2–4.

Chapter 9   A natural history of evil

1   Here quoted from Frederick Davies's English translation, *The Gods
    Will Have Blood*, Penguin Classics, 1979.
2   See Milan Kundera, *The Curtain: An Essay in Seven Parts*, trans.
    Linda Asher, Faber & Faber, 2007, pp. 92, 123, 110.
3   See Émile Cioran, *Précis de decomposition*, Gallimard, 1949.
4   Friedrich Nietzsche, *The Antichrist*, trans. Anthony M. Ludovici,
    Prometheus Books, 2000, p. 4.
5   Friedrich Nietzsche, *Ecce Homo*, trans. R. J. Hollingdale, Penguin,
    1979, p. 97.
6   Friedrich Nietzsche, *Thus Spoke Zarathustra*, trans. R. J. Hollingdale,
    Penguin, 2003, p. 204.
7   The subtitle of Philip Zimbardo's *The Lucifer Effect*, Rider, 2009.
8   Littell, *The Kindly Ones*. The original French title of *Les Bienveillantes*,
    and the title of the German translation, *Die Wohlgesinnten*, seem to
    convey the intended interpretation better than the English transla-
    tion. A title such as 'The Well-wishers', or better still 'The Benevolent',
    would be much more faithful to the original intention.
9   To paraphrase Brecht: 'First a guzzle, morality later'.
10 See Hannah Arendt, *The Origins of Totalitarianism*, Deutsch, 1986,
    p. 338.
11 Hannah Arendt, *Eichmann in Jerusalem: A Report on the Banality
    of Evil*, Viking, 1964, p. 35.
12 Littell, *The Kindly Ones*, pp. 569–70.
13 Ibid., p. 565.
14 John Steiner, 'The SS yesterday and today: a sociopsychological
    view', in Joel E. Dinsdale (ed.), *Survivors, Victims and Perpetrators*,
    Hemisphere, 1980, p. 431.
15 See Craig Haney, Curtis Banks and Philip Zimbardo, 'Interpersonal
    dynamics in a simulated prison', *International Journal of Criminology
    and Penology*, 1973, pp. 69–97.
16 For full discussion, see Zygmunt Bauman, *Modernity and the
    Holocaust*, Polity, 1989, ch. 6.
17 See Christopher R. Browning, *Ordinary Men: Reserve Police
    Battalion 101 and the Final Solution in Poland*, Penguin, 2001.
18 W. G. Sebald, *On the Natural History of Destruction*, trans. Anthea
    Bell, Hamish Hamilton, 2003.

19   Ibid., p. 65.

20   Ibid., p. 18.

21   See Günther Anders, *Wir Eichmannsöhne* (1964, 1988), here translated from the French edition, *Nous, fils d'Eichmann*, Rivages, 2003, p. 47.

22   See Hermann Knell, *To Destroy a City: Strategic Bombing and Its Human Consequences in World War II*, Da Capo Press, 2003, particularly pp. 25 and 330–1.

23   Enzo Traverso, *La Violence nazie. Une généalogie européenne*, La Fabrique, 2003.

24   Anders, *Nous, fils d'Eichmann*, p. 108.

25   In Joseph Roth, *Juden auf Wanderschaft*, here quoted from Michael Hoffmann's translation, *The Wandering Jews*, Granta Books, 2001, p. 125.

26   See Günther Anders, *Wenn ich verzweifelt bin, was geh't mich an?* (1977), here quoted from the French translation, *Et si je suis désespéré, que voulez-vous que j'y fasse?*, Éditions Allia, 2007, pp. 65–6.

27   See Günther Anders, *Der Mann auf der Brucke*, C. H. Beck, 1959, p. 144.

28   See Günther Anders, *Le Temps de la fin*, L'Herne, 2007 (original 1960), pp. 52–3.

29   See Günther Anders, *Die Antiquiertheit des Menschen. Über die Seele im Zeitalter der zweiten industriellen Revolution*, C. H. Beck, 1956, here translated from the French edition, *L'Obsolescence de l'Homme. Sur l'âme à l'époque de la deuxième révolution industrielle*, Encyclopédie des Nuisances, 2002, pp. 37–40.

30   See Anders, *Et si je suis désespéré*, pp. 67–8.

31   See Anders, *Wenn ich verzweifelt bin*, p. 100.

32   Ibid., p. 92.

Chapter 10   *Wir arme Leut'* . . .

This chapter was first published in German as an essay in the booklet accompanying the Bavarian State Opera's 2008–9 production of Alban Berg's opera *Wozzeck*.

1   Polly Toynbee and David Walker, 'Meet the rich', *Guardian*, 4 Aug. 2008.

2   See Dennis Smith, *Globalization: The Hidden Agenda*, Polity, 2006, p. 38.

3   Ibid., p. 37.

Chapter 11   Sociology: whence and whither?

This chapter is based on a background paper prepared for acceptance of the Distinguished Contribution to Sociological Theory Award of the International Studies Association at the Seventeenth ISA World Congress of Sociology held in Gothenburg in July 2010.

Index